FRENCH *Beans*

PHOTOGRAPHS Steve Sando

PHOTOGRAPHS on pages 22–23, 30–31, 46–47, and 102–103 © Getty Images, page 68 and fabric texture © Shutterstock

BOOK DESIGN Meghan Hildebrand

EDITOR Julia Newberry

COPYEDITOR Anita Epler Crotty

Copyright 2018 Rancho Gordo Press. All rights reserved. No part of this book may be reproduced in any form without written permission from the publisher.

ISBN: 978-0-692-16011-4

Printed in China.

FSC — MIX Paper from responsible sources FSC® C016973 www.fsc.org

Rancho Gordo Press
1924 Yajome St, Napa, CA 94559
www.ranchogordo.com

FRENCH *Beans*

EXPLORING THE BEAN CUISINE OF FRANCE

by
GEORGEANNE BRENNAN

RANCHO GORDO PRESS

TABLE OF CONTENTS

Introduction — 8
The History and Use of Beans in France — 10
French Bean Profiles — 13
Labels of Quality in France — 25
Cooking Dried Beans — 26
The Essential French Pantry — 29

CHAPTER 1
SPREADS, DIPS, and APPETIZERS

Buttered Garlic Toasts with White Beans and Crispy Pork — 32
Black Bean Hummus — 34
Green Lentil and Goat Cheese Spread with Chives — 35
White Bean and Chorizo Tartines — 37
Fried Panisse Batons — 38
Spicy Roasted Chickpeas — 39
Creamy White Bean and Anchovy Dip — 40
Smoked Salmon and White Bean Rillettes — 42
Haricots de Soissons Beans with Maroilles Cheese — 43
Chickpea Beignets — 45

CHAPTER 2
SALADS

Salade Niçoise: From Simple Southern Meal to International Favorite — 49
  Salade Niçoise with Cranberry Beans and Tuna Confit — 50
  Salade Niçoise with Seared Tuna and White Beans — 51
  Classic Salade Niçoise — 52
White Bean, Watercress, and Pickled Herring Salad — 54
White Beans with Lardons, Red Peppers, and Piment d'Espelette — 56
Salad of Salt Cod and White Beans — 57
White Beans with Arugula, Prosciutto, and Parmesan Vinaigrette — 59
Duck Breast, Lentil, and Green Herb Salad — 60
Smoked Trout, Shaved Celery, and White Beans with Tarragon Vinaigrette — 61
Salade Mexicaine — 62
Grilled Calamari with Coco Beans and Charred Tomatoes — 65
Chickpeas with Prosciutto, Black Olives, and Cherry Tomatoes — 66

CHAPTER 3
GRATINS, ROASTS, and OTHER MAIN DISHES

The Lamb-and-Flageolet Love Affair	71
Roast Leg of Lamb with Garlic, Herbs, and Flageolet Beans	72
Tomato-Braised Lamb Shanks with Flageolet Beans	74
Lamb Stew with Flageolet Beans	76
Gratin of Leeks and White Beans with Gruyère	78
Hachis Parmentier	79
Gratin of Cranberry Beans, Sweet Peppers, and Toulouse Sausage	81
Chickpea and Lamb Gratin with Harissa	82
Braised Chicken Thighs with Cranberry Beans and Basil	83
Basque-Style Beans with Standing Pork Rib Roast	84
Rosemary White Beans with Beef and Cherry Tomato Brochettes	87
Sea Bass on a Bed of Puréed White Beans	88
Papillotes of Sole, White Beans, and Spinach with Saffron Sauce	91
Garlic Shrimp with White Beans and Sauce Verte	92
The Mystique of Cassoulet	95
A Grand Cassoulet with Lamb, Pork, and Duck Confit	96
Cassoulet, More-or-Less Toulouse-Style	98
Slightly Short-Cut Cassoulet	100

CHAPTER 4
SOUPS and STEWS

Soupe au Pistou and Its Seasonal Variations	105
Classic Summer Soupe au Pistou	106
Springtime Soupe au Pistou	107
Fall Soupe au Pistou	108
Loubia	110
Cream of Fennel and White Bean Soup	112
Ragout of Chickpeas and Chorizo	113
Couscous Garni	114
Carbonnade with Lingot du Nord Beans	116
Garbure	118
Breton Beans	119
Périgord-Style Duck Soup with White Beans	121
Index	122
Acknowledgements	128

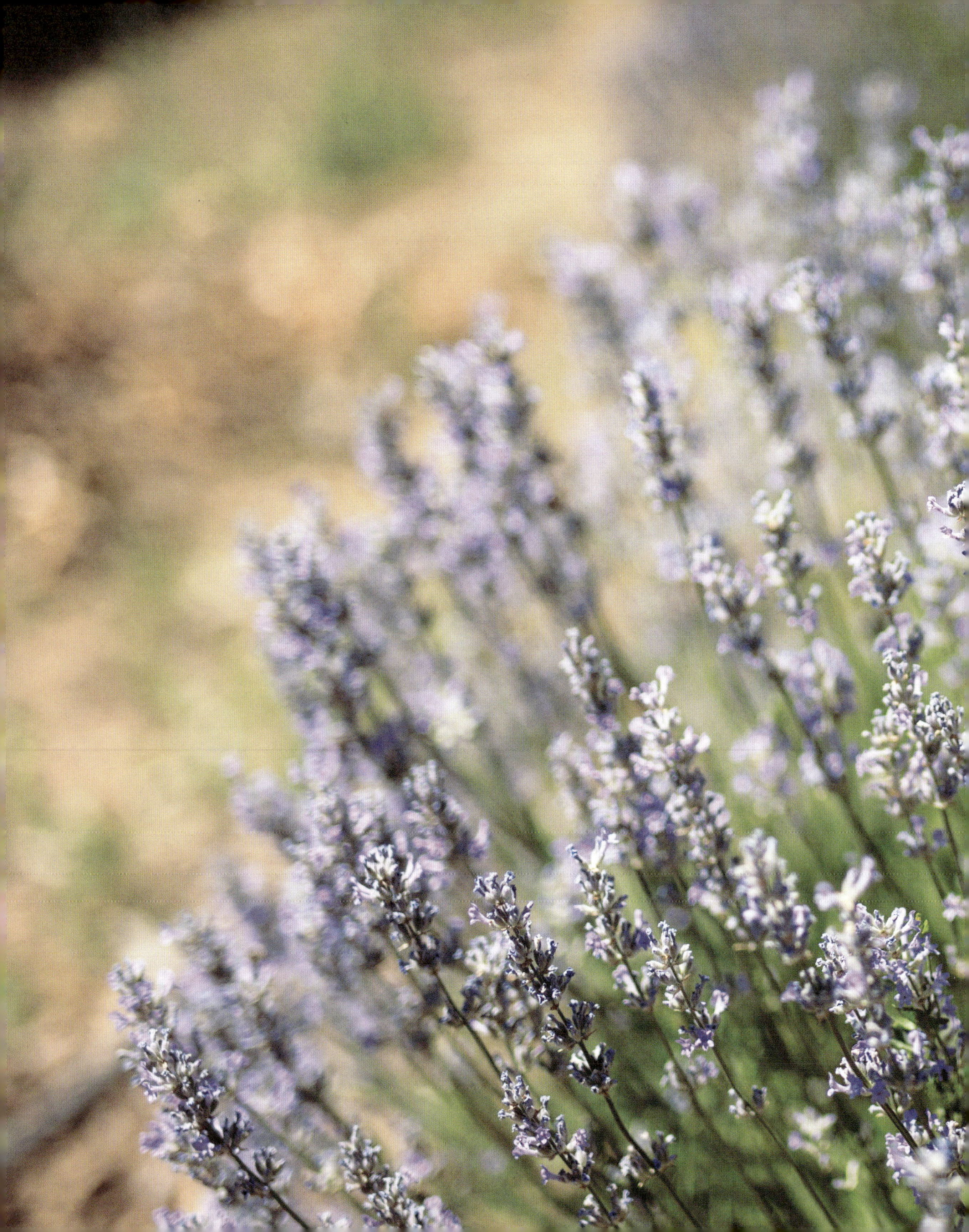

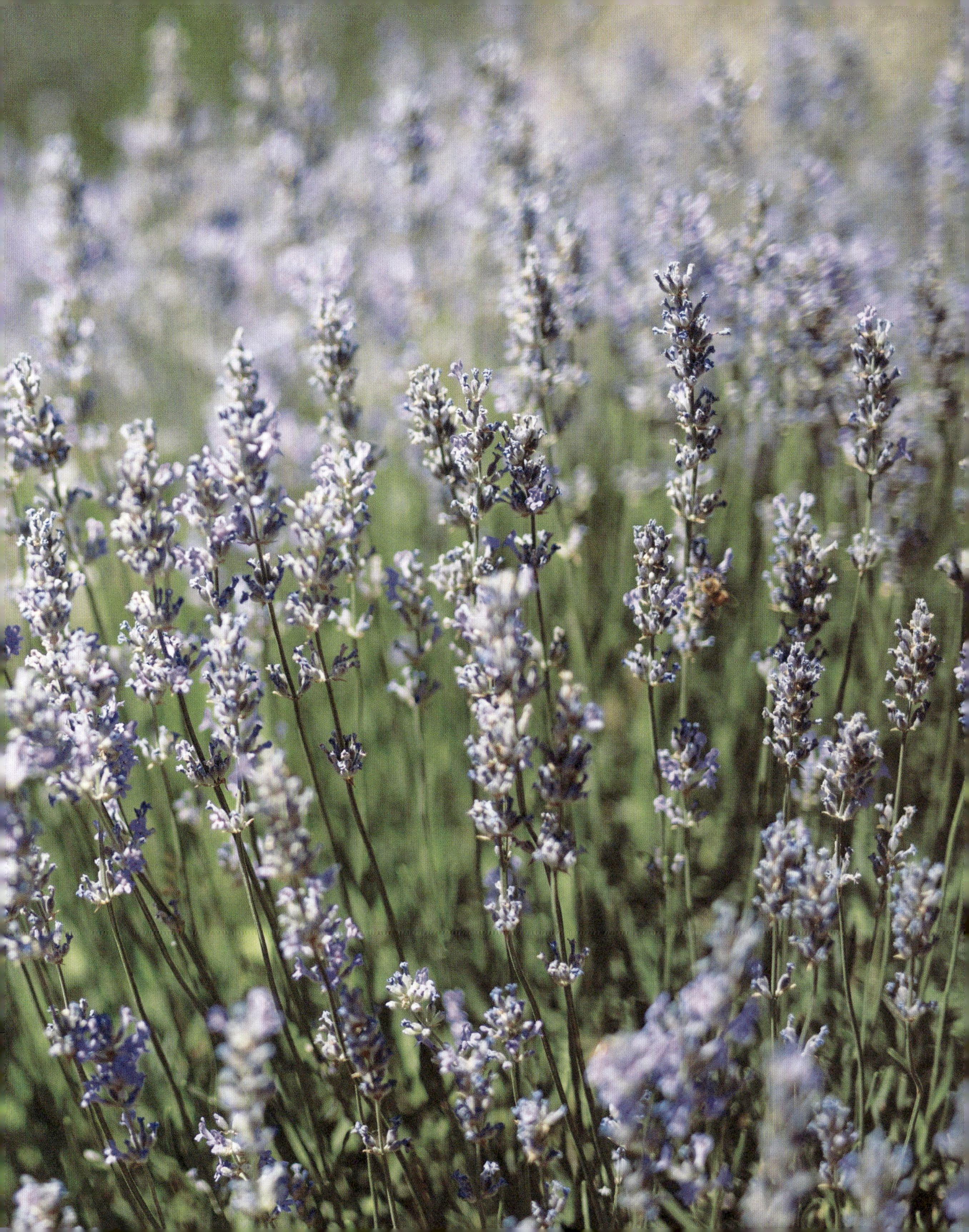

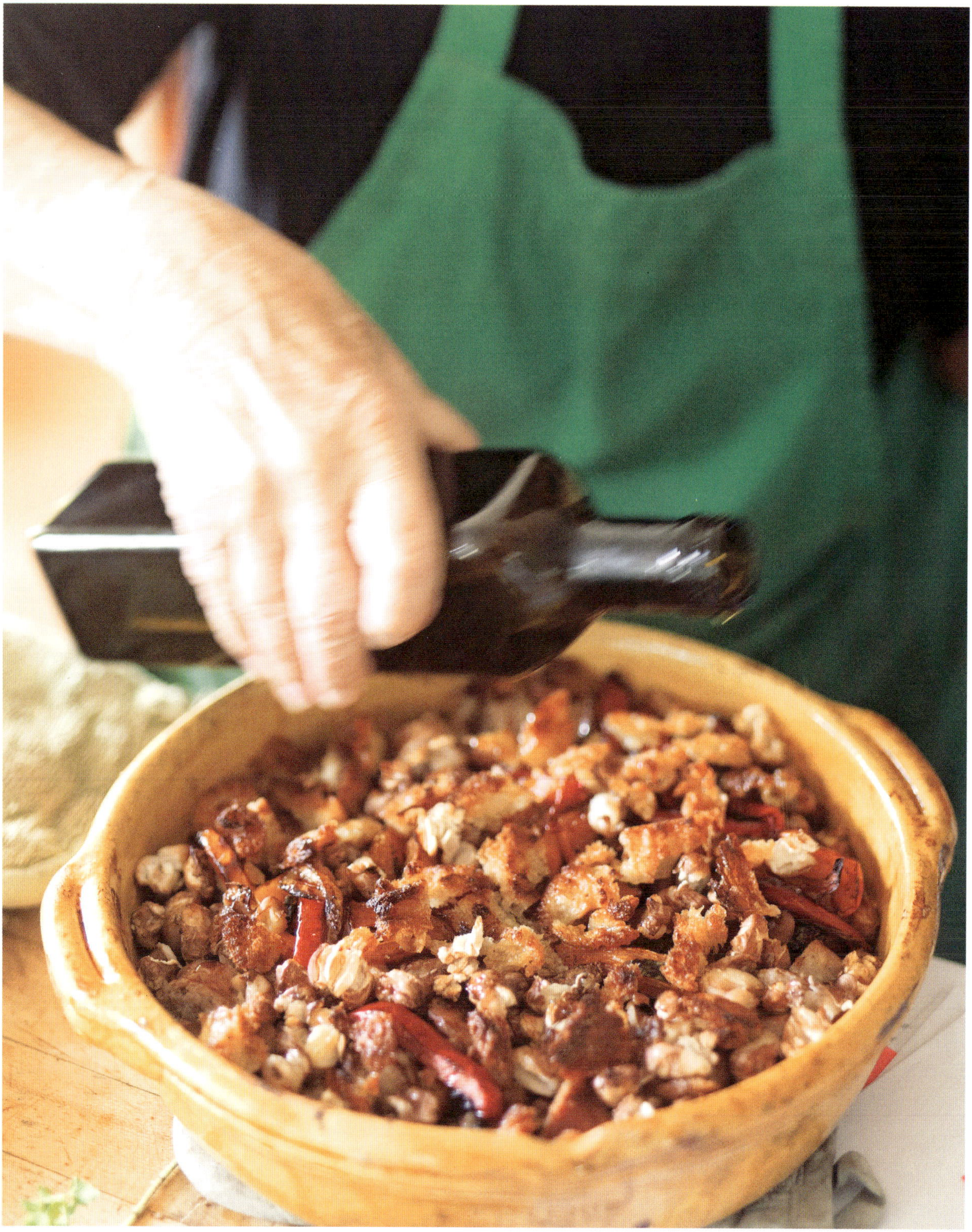

INTRODUCTION

At a dinner party one night, I made an off-the-cuff remark to Georgeanne Brennan about how, once you got past cassoulet, beans were fairly limited in French cuisine. I'm sure she bristled, but she was far too polite to show it. She took a moment, and then proceeded to list dozens and dozens of French dishes — both classic and little-known — featuring beans. I quickly realized how silly my comment had been.

My company, Rancho Gordo, specializes in heirloom beans but most of the recipes we've shared with customers have focused on Mexican, Italian, and California cuisines. France wasn't registering for me beyond cassoulet, and yet Georgeanne could rattle off a whole book's worth of recipes and bean culture. At first, I was hungry. Then I was intrigued.

I asked Georgeanne if we could collaborate, and she quickly agreed. We decided to create the French bean book that we'd want for our own kitchens. I dislike the word "authentic," but we both felt that the recipes should truly reflect the meals that Georgeanne has enjoyed in France, and that we should not compromise the spirit of a dish for the sake of convenience (or to sell more beans).

It turns out that good home cooking in France is the same as good home cooking everywhere: simple to make and easy to love.

I learned two important lessons during the making of this book: Always listen to Georgeanne Brennan, and never take France for granted!

—Steve Sando
RANCHO GORDO

THE HISTORY *and* USE OF *Beans* IN FRANCE

To some degree, beans have been cultivated in France since they first made their appearance in Europe in the 1500s, after being brought back by colonial explorers. By the mid-1800s, famous French horticulturists and seed purveyors M. Vilmorin and M. Andrieux listed more than 40 different varieties of New World beans in their monumental book, *The Vegetable Garden*. Some of these, including Flageolet, Coco Blanc, Coco Rouge, and Haricot de Soissons, remain in commercial production in France.

Prior to the introduction of New World beans, French cooks were well acquainted with the fava bean, a different species known as long ago as the time of the pharaohs. Chickpeas have been cultivated in Southern Europe, North Africa, and the Middle East for thousands of years, and remain an important food in France today. Chickpeas — and lentils, which are also not beans — are still widely used in France and prepared in ways that are similar to beans. Conversely, dried fava beans have declined in favor of the New World beans, though fresh favas continue to be widely popular.

Some of the beans described in this book are not available in the United States, but I include them here because they're deeply representative of the French attachment to local products as an important part of their patrimony. When the traditional recipe calls for an unavailable French bean, I suggest substitutions; in many cases, alternate beans available here in the United States — such as the Alubia Blanca, Flageolet, Cannellini, Cassoulet, white and red Kidney beans, and black beans — are used in France as well. Other substitutions are notably similar to French beans in size and use — such as Royal Coronas when a large, white bean is needed; or the Cassoulet bean, the American-grown equivalent of the French Tarbais. In general, white beans of varying types and sizes — such as the Lingot or white Kidney bean, Coco Blanc, plus the green Flageolet — dominate in France. There is some use of red and black beans, notably in French-style chile con carne or Mexican-style salads; I've included recipes for these, although they are not common French beans.

Some beans in France are also used *demi-sec* — what Americans call shelling beans. The outside pod is partially dried and the beans inside are still tender, and not fully mature. These *demi-sec* beans come into the marketplace from late July into September, depending on the type of bean and the weather, and this short season is highly anticipated. The beans, still in their pods, can be purchased by the kilo, but the traditionalists buy them in 10-kilo (22-pound) bags, sometimes directly from the producer at the farm, to shell and to use right away. Others will shell the beans then freeze or can them, as they are considered a seasonal delicacy.

In writing this book with Steve Sando of Rancho Gordo — well-recognized for his bean expertise — I felt it was important to explore the ways French cooks use beans, both in traditional and contemporary dishes beyond the familiar cassoulet and, where appropriate, to provide some history of both the beans and the dishes. Not surprisingly, you'll find that the hallmarks of French country cooking — herbs, seasonal vegetables, and regional meats, fowl, and fish — are to be found equally in their bean cookery as elsewhere. Thyme and winter savory are French favorites to season beans, along with the classic *bouquet garni*: a bundle of bay leaf, parsley, and thyme.

—Georgeanne Brennan

FLAGEOLET

FRENCH BEAN PROFILES

FLAGEOLET

The Flageolet bean is a small, kidney-shaped variety that is pale green or white. It is said to have come to France with Catherine de' Médicis, who had received them as a gift from Pope Clement VII. She married Henry II in 1533, but the beans became famous only when a French market grower, Gabriel Chevrier, discovered a plant with greener leaves and pods growing among his Flageolet beans in a Parisian suburb. The beans inside the pods were pastel green as well, unlike the other Flageolets he was growing. He named the new variety Flageolet Chevrier Vert, and, in 1878, he started selling the dried beans. They were an immediate hit with the chefs of Paris restaurants, and home cooks followed suit. Today, the pale green Flageolet, produced primarily in Brittany and the north, is the most popular bean in France. The variety has been proposed for the European Label Rouge, a designation of place and quality (see page 25).

The bean has a mild, slightly meaty flavor with a creamy interior and a thin skin, and holds its shape when cooked to just tender to the bite. If overcooked, the skin will burst. This trait has given Flageolets an undeserved reputation for being tricky to cook.

Flageolet beans have become inseparable from the leg of lamb (page 71), and are served with lamb dishes of all kinds, but they can also be puréed, served in salads, and used to accompany meats beyond the classic lamb. In the north of France, Flageolet beans are often used in cassoulet instead of the Tarbais bean that's traditional in the southwest.

HARICOT DE SOISSONS

Haricot de Soissons beans are the largest of the French varieties, a good inch or more long, with a plump profile. They're popular for salads, gratins, and any other dishes where a large, meaty bean is desirable. Like so many foods of France, this bean is the subject of legends. One popular tale holds that, during the Hundred Years' War, when the people of Soissons fled the city because of the plague, seeds fell from their belongings. When people finally returned to the city, the surrounding fields were thick with bean plants. Another legend from the 19th century has the beans sprouting from the gutters of the cathedral, and covering the cathedral walls with their hanging, pod-laden vines.

Today, this bean is grown primarily near Soissons and Reims, in the northeast corner of France, in relatively small amounts.

TARBAIS

After the Flageolet bean, the Tarbais bean is probably the best-known French variety because of its strong association with cassoulet (page 95). This medium-size bean holds its shape during the long cooking of this most-famous dish, readily absorbing the flavors of the other ingredients. These same qualities make this variety equally good for other dishes, such as soups and salads, and as a general all-round bean. The vining plants are grown in and around the commune of Tarbes in southwestern France, and are traditionally planted along with corn, which acts to stake the vines. The beans are hand-harvested, a labor-intensive process that's part of why the beans have earned the Label Rouge designation as well as the geographical protection known as IGP. The American-grown equivalent of the French Tarbais bean is known as the Cassoulet bean.

COCO BEANS

Coco beans are grown extensively throughout France by market growers, small farmers, and home gardeners. The nearly round beans are extremely popular as *demi-sec* shelling beans. Come July, great mounds of pods start appearing in the open markets, farm stands, and supermarkets. There are two main types: white Coco Blanc and red Coco Rouge. In two areas of France, the Coco beans are grown using traditional methods of cultivation and harvest: Coco de Paimpol in Brittany, and Coco de Pamiers in southwestern France.

COCO BLANC

Rounded, and varying in size from very small to medium-small, Coco Blanc beans are sold in their creamy yellow pods in summer and early fall — while they are still in the shelling or *demi-sec* stage — and then later sold shelled and dried.

COCO DE PAIMPOL

This is the famous bean of Brittany, named after the coastal town of Paimpol. The story has it that a sailor, returning from Argentina, brought seeds of the small, round bean back to France with him, and the beans were first planted around 1928. During summer and fall, Coco de Paimpol beans are sold in the pods by the sackfull at local farms and farmers' markets. People buy large quantities of the beans, shell them, and then freeze the beans to use over the rest of the year. The beans have an unusual, nutty flavor that goes exceptionally well with the shellfish of the region. Coco de Paimpol has earned the coveted Label Rouge designation, as well as both AOC and AOP protections for regional products.

TARBAIS

ALUBIA BLANCA

COCO DE PAMIERS

These small Coco beans have long been grown in the southwest of France on the plain of Ariège, south of the plain of Lauragrais, not far from Carcassonne, where the Lingot de Mazère is also grown. Coco de Pamiers beans are used as the base of Mounjetado, the Ariègeois version of cassoulet. They almost disappeared from cultivation in the 1990s, overtaken in popularity by the Lingot bean, until an aspiring group of farmers banded together and began growing the local Coco beans and promoting them in local restaurants, fairs, and trade shows.

COCO ROUGE

Coco Rouge beans are also known as Cranberry beans and Borlotti beans. Many different varieties are cultivated all over France, especially by market growers and home gardeners. The pods are shades of red streaked with creamy white. The beans inside are creamy white with purplish veining. Dried, the beans are buff-pink, or brown and marbled with red or mahogany; they have a deep, meaty flavor. Fresh or dried, they are considered, like the Coco Blanc, an important ingredient for Soupe au Pistou (page 105).

ALUBIA BLANCA

Alubia Blanca, a smallish, white Kidney bean, is associated with Spanish cooking, as is the famous Alubia Rojo bean of Tolosa in the Basque region. France imports these beans in quantity, and they are often sold simply as white beans, or *haricots blancs*, as they are excellent, all-purpose beans for any sort of dish.

HARICOT MAÏS DU BÉARN

Seeds for this variety of white bean have been passed down through the generations in southwestern France near the Pyrenees. It is called the *maïs* (corn) bean because it has been traditionally planted next to corn stalks to support its climbing vines. The beans are used both *demi-sec* and dried, and are the classic bean for Garbure, a hearty regional soup (page 118). Cream-colored and largish, it is about the size of a Tarbais bean.

LINGOT BEANS

These medium-small, brilliant white beans are called Lingot because of their ingot shape — thin and more straight-sided and blunt-ended — resembling Cannellini beans more than the rounded kidney shape of Flageolet and Tarbais beans. Some Lingot beans are associated with specific regions and take the name of their origin area. Others are sold simply as Haricots Lingot. However, they are also known generically as white Kidney beans, in spite of the ingot shape. These multipurpose beans hold their form when cooked; they have thin skins and creamy interiors.

Some varieties of Lingot beans have been grown in various regions of France since the mid-1800s. After declining production in the mid-20th century, they are now experiencing a resurgence; in two specific areas, they have earned Label Rouge and IGP classifications. Because of the small, local production of Lingot beans, they are rarely found outside of France and much of their consumption remains regional. Lingot beans are one of two main types used for cassoulet in France.

MOGETTE DE VENDÉE

Also known as Mojette, this Lingot variety is grown in the Vendée region of west-central France, just south of the Loire River and bordering the Atlantic. Mogette beans have been awarded Label Rouge and IGP designation.

LINGOT DU NORD

This bean is cultivated in the region of Hauts-de-France (formerly Nord-Pas-de-Calais and Picardy), near the Belgian border, primarily in the Plaine de la Lys, which stretches along the Lys River. Records note this variety being grown as far back as the mid-1800s. The beans are still hand-harvested, and entire plants are tossed onto cone-shaped wooden structures to further dry. When covered with the drying beans, the structures look like haystacks. The beans are valued for their thin skin, creamy melting interiors, and classic bean flavor. They have earned Label Rouge and IGP designations.

LINGOT DE MAZÈRES

Grown in Mazères, a commune in the Ariège department not far from Carcassonne, this is the preferred bean used in that city's version of cassoulet.

LINGOT DE LAURAGAIS

This Lingot bean is produced on the Lauragais plain near Castelnaudary — considered to be the birthplace of cassoulet — and it is considered the classic bean for that city's famous dish. They are also sometimes labeled Lingot de Castelnaudary.

CHICKPEAS

Fresh or dried, whole, puréed, or milled into flour, the chickpea has long been a staple of Mediterranean regions. It was one of the earliest vegetables cultivated by humans, dating back more than 7,000 years. Although the chickpea originated in the Middle East, its cultivation spread throughout the Mediterranean and on to Africa, and finally making its way to the New World by way of European sailors.

CHICKPEAS

LENTILS

In France, chickpeas — *pois chiches* — have become so associated with Marseille and Nice that they are considered part of the culinary patrimony. Chickpeas are most notably used in two local dishes there: *panisse* and *socca*. Both are made with nothing more than chickpea flour, water, salt, and olive oil. *Panisse* is thick like polenta and served sliced and fried. *Socca* is cooked on flat, round hot plates, and is thin like a crepe. In the 1800s, women made and sold hot *socca* from pushcarts found along the port and streets of Marseille; in Nice, the *socca* vendors were found in stalls around the marketplace at La Saleya, as they are today. Chickpeas are still grown today in the regions around Nice, in the department of Var, and in the Southwest.

Chickpeas, also called Garbanzo beans, have a firm, meaty texture and a delicate, nutlike flavor that makes them a good addition to soups and stews. They can also be cooked on their own, then seasoned, roasted and fried. In North African countries of Morocco, Algeria, and Tunisia —colonized by France— chickpeas feature largely in such dishes as tagines and couscous.

LENTILS

France is famous for its small, dark-green, almost slate-black lentils, called French green lentils. Although grown in many regions of France, including Provence, the heart of the production is the commune of Le Puy-en-Velay in south-central France, where they have been grown for more than 2,000 years. These tiny gems, Lentilles Vertes du Puy, are grown in volcanic soil, and have a peppery, mineral taste; they have been awarded AOC and AOP protections. The region of Berry, not far from Paris, also, has received Label Rouge recognition for the qualities of its French green lentils. French green lentils hold their shape when cooked, which makes them ideal for salads and other dishes where texture, as well as flavor, is important.

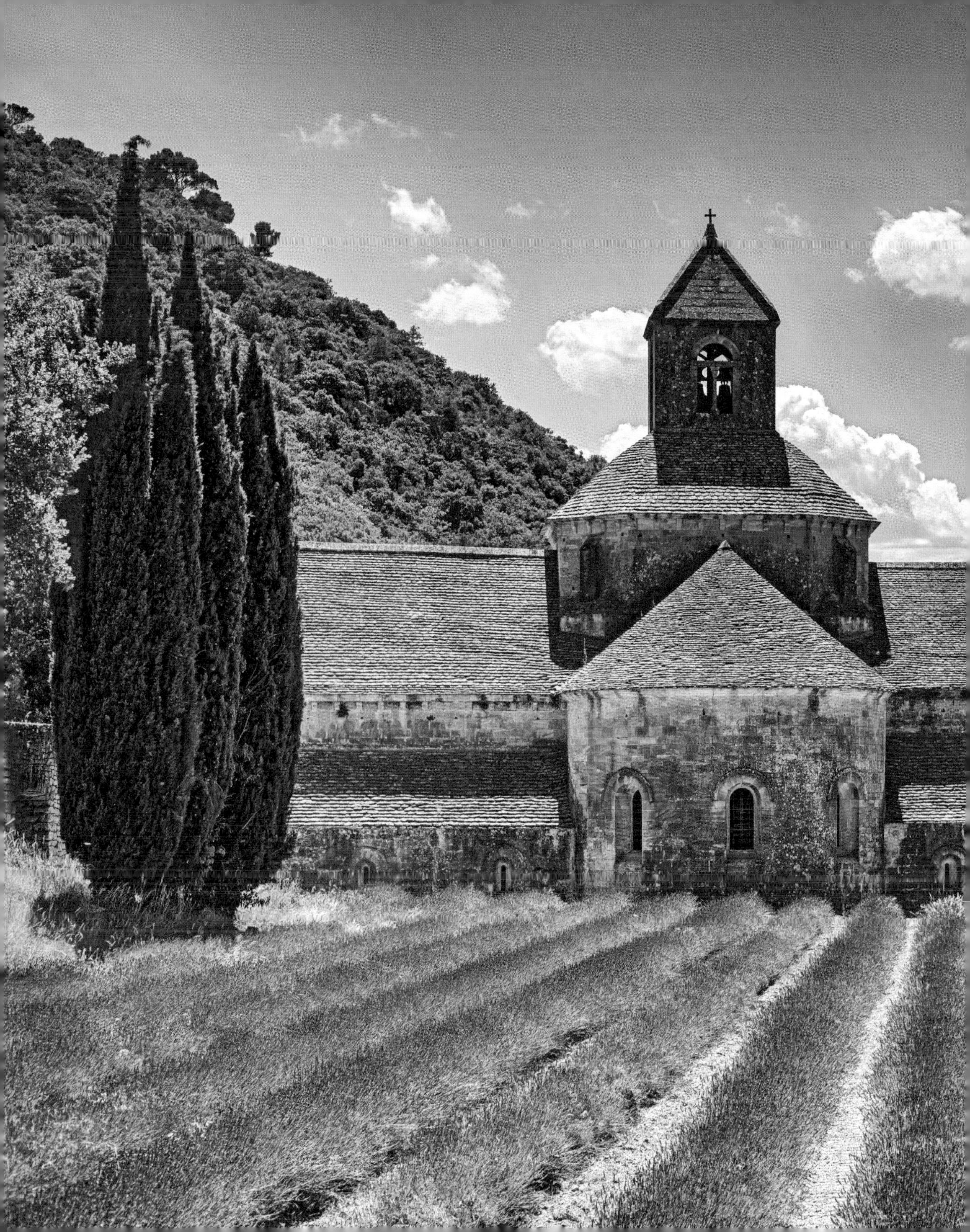

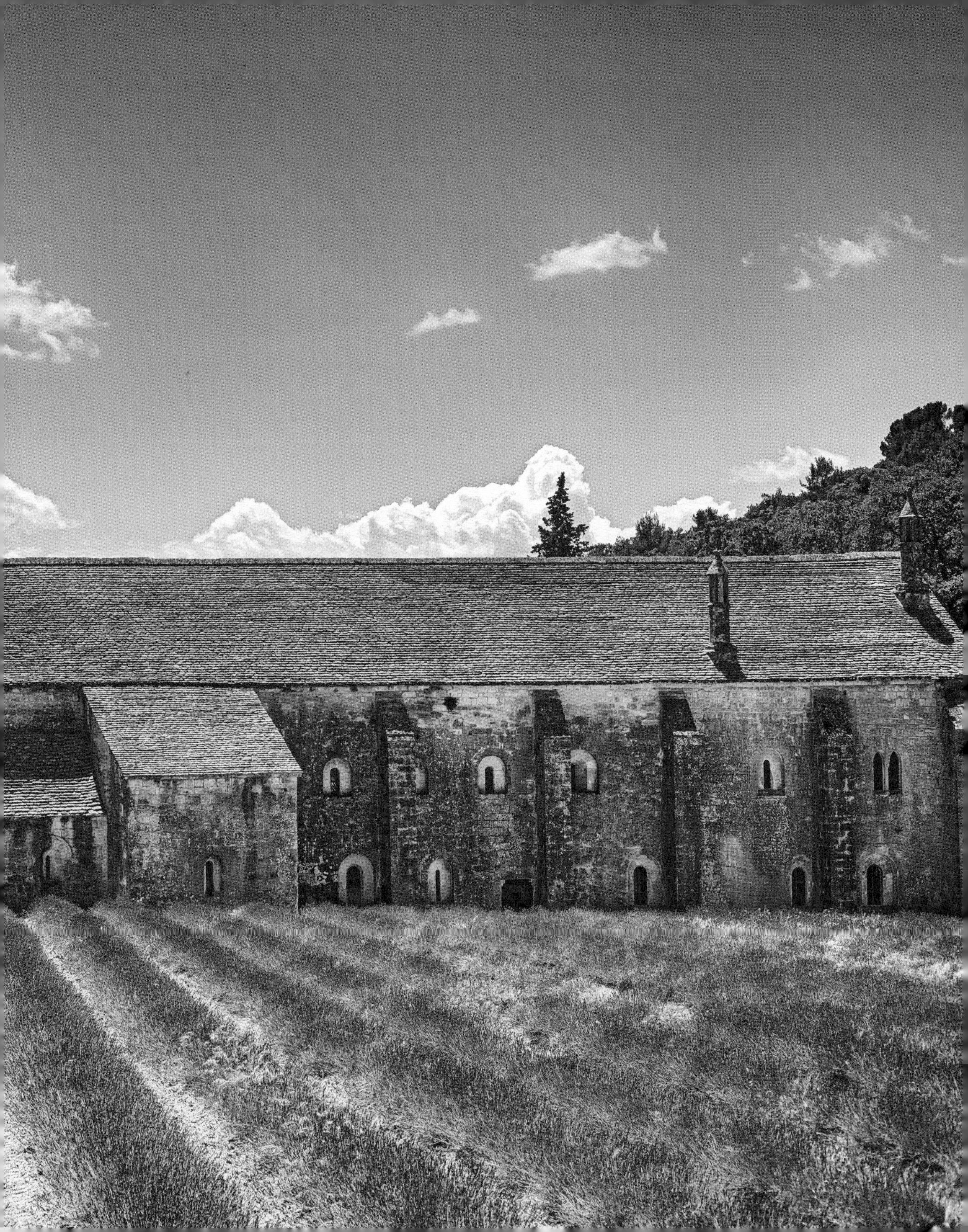

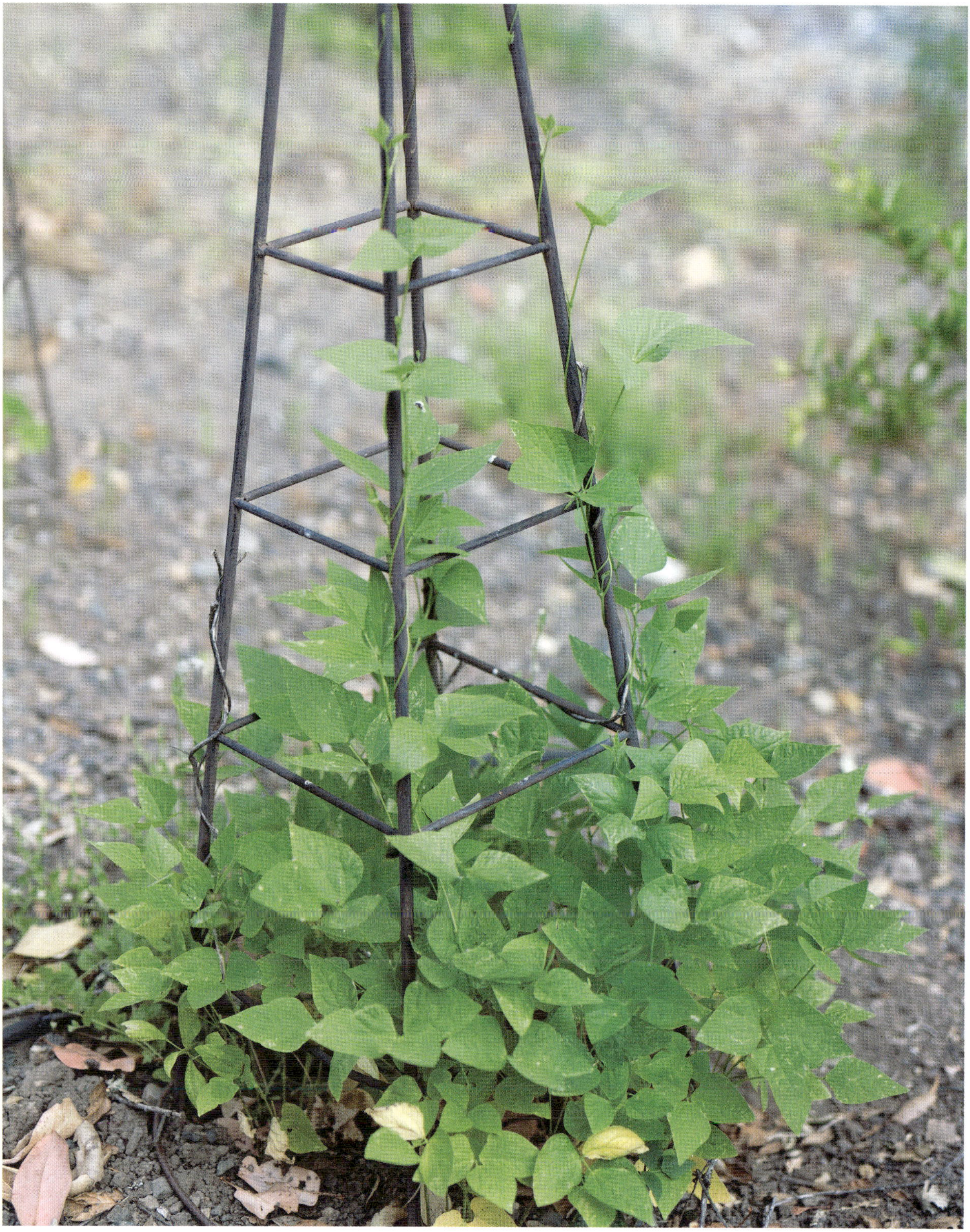

LABELS OF QUALITY IN FRANCE

AOC *(Appellation d'Origine Contrôlée)*

This designation recognizes product that has been produced, processed, and developed according to specific regulations established by the French government; it is tied to a specific geographic region.

AOP *(Appellation d'Origine Protégée)*

This designation recognizes a product for which all of the production stages (production, processing, and development) are carried out according to recognized expertise within the same geographical area that gives its characteristics to the product, according to the French government. This label is gradually replacing AOC as the top designation for a product, including wines.

IGP *(Indication Géographique Protégée)*

This European quality seal designates a product whose characteristics are linked to a geographical area where at least its production or its processing takes place according to precise conditions.

LABEL ROUGE

This official designation from the French Ministry of Agriculture guarantees that the product you're buying offers superior quality, or is made according to more rigorous standards, than one that does not bear the label.

COOKING DRIED BEANS

Soaking dried beans can speed up the cooking process and help beans cook more evenly, but it's not necessary if you start with good-quality beans and use them within two years of harvest. Adding broth, seasonings, or vegetables will make beans more flavorful, but I generally cook them very simply, adding a bay leaf while simmering, and salting near the end. No matter your source for dried beans, it's always a good idea to pick through them for small stones and debris, and rinse them well before soaking or cooking.

1 pound dried beans, picked over and rinsed

1 bay leaf

Sea salt

Soak beans for 4 to 6 hours. (If you don't have time to soak your beans, don't fret. Go ahead and cook them unsoaked, knowing it will take a bit longer.)

In a large pot over medium-high heat, add beans and their soaking water, plus enough water to cover beans by a couple of inches. Add bay leaf.

Bring the pot to a hard boil. Cook for 10 minutes, then reduce heat to a gentle simmer before covering. Open and close the lid occasionally, or keep it ajar, to help control heat and allow some evaporation. Bean broth will taste best if it has a chance to breathe and reduce a little.

After about an hour, start checking beans for doneness. If the broth starts getting low, add boiling water to keep beans completely covered.

Once beans are nearly tender, add salt. Go easy at first, and taste beans after a bit more cooking; it takes a while for them to absorb salt.

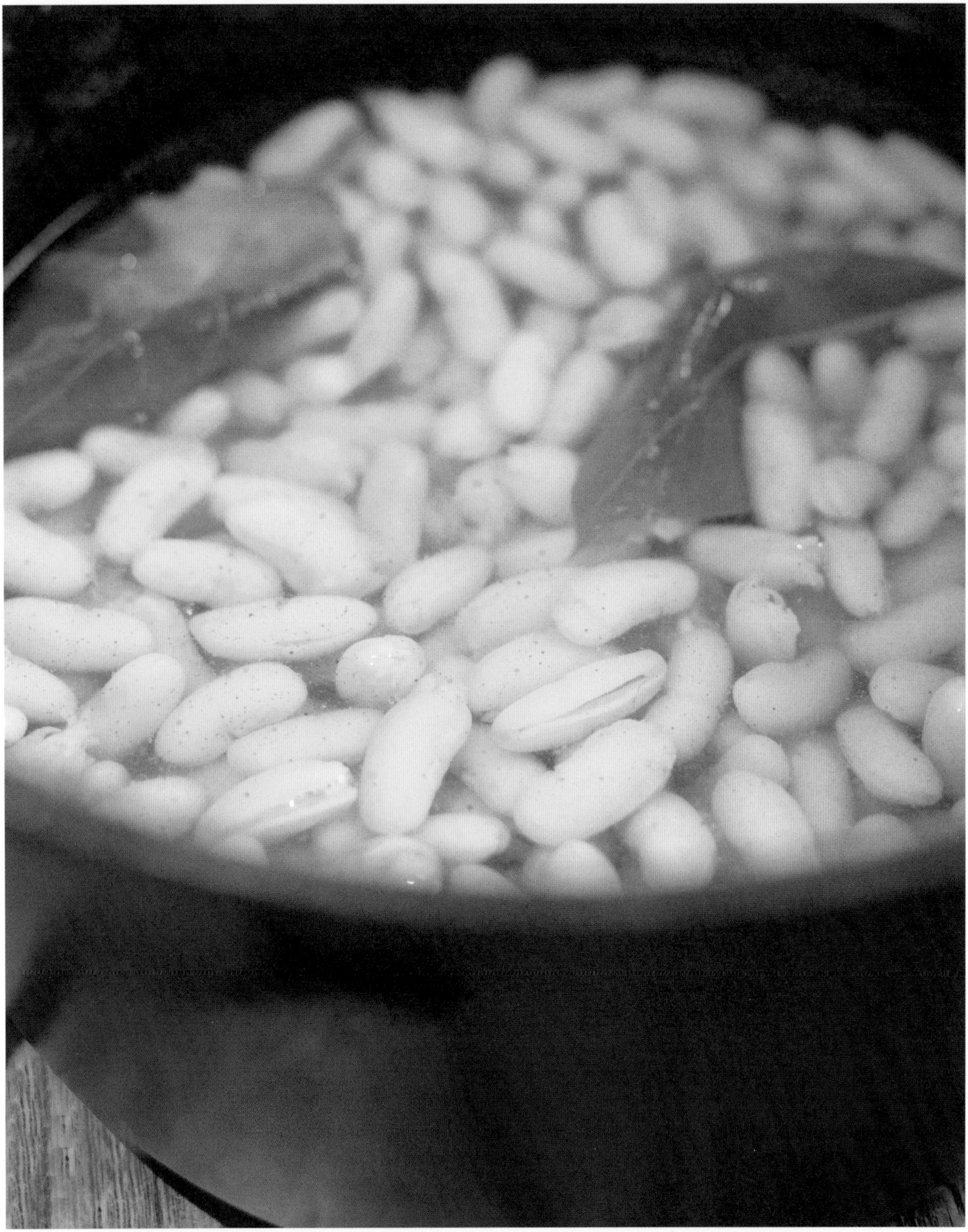

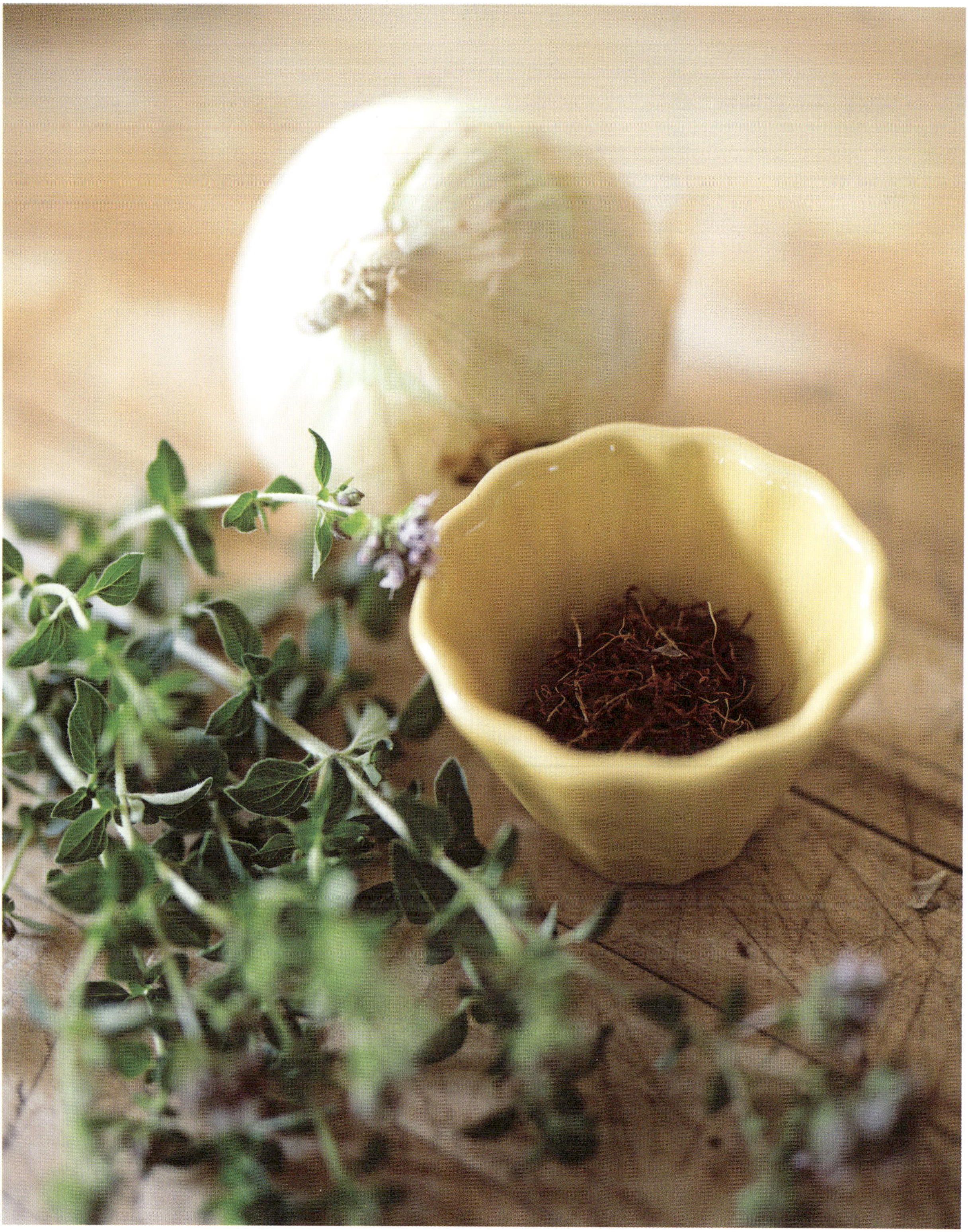

THE ESSENTIAL FRENCH PANTRY

Keeping a handful of good-quality ingredients on hand makes it easier to prepare French-inspired bean dishes throughout the year. Tending a small garden of fresh herbs is another great way to ensure you have classic French bean seasonings at the ready.

AROMATICS

Carrot
Celery
Fennel
Garlic
Leeks
Onion
Shallot

FRESH HERBS

Basil
Chives
Flat-leaf parsley
Oregano
Rosemary
Tarragon
Thyme
Winter savory

OILS AND VINEGARS

Extra-virgin olive oil
Walnut oil
Pistachio oil
Red wine vinegar
Champagne vinegar
White wine vinegar

JARRED AND CANNED INGREDIENTS

Anchovies packed in olive oil: A classic garnish for Salade Niçoise, the key ingredient in *anchoiade*, and a great pantry snack.

Dijon mustard: A must for thickening and flavoring vinaigrettes, and the secret spicy kick in carbonnade.

Olives of all kinds: A lovely addition to salads, and a no-fuss appetizer or snack.

Capers: These small, briny buds add a complex bite to salads and sauces.

Harissa: North African chile sauce essential for couscous garni and other Moroccan-influenced dishes.

Canned tomatoes: A tin or jar adds a bright note to gratins and stews.

Tomato paste: Lends a concentrated tomato flavor that pairs well with spicy, meaty recipes.

Homemade chicken, beef, or vegetable stock: Make in bulk and freeze, or substitute good-quality low-salt commercial broth in a pinch.

DRIED HERBS AND SPICES

Sea salt: Unrefined salts contain trace minerals and contribute to more complex flavors in food.

Freshly ground black pepper: Pre-ground pepper, like any spice, begins losing flavor almost immediately.

Bay leaves: A key aromatic for beans and stocks.

Herbes de Provence: This blend of Provençal herbs — usually savory, marjoram, rosemary, thyme, oregano, and sometimes lavender — adds a unique accent.

Oregano: A key Mediterranean herb, often found in ragouts and hearty gratins.

Rosemary: When dried, this classic herb shares a natural affinity with white beans and other winter fare.

Piment d'Espelette: Ground dried chile peppers from the Basque region bring a gentle heat.

Saffron: A worthy extravagance; a few threads lend color and earthy flavor to seafood and sauces.

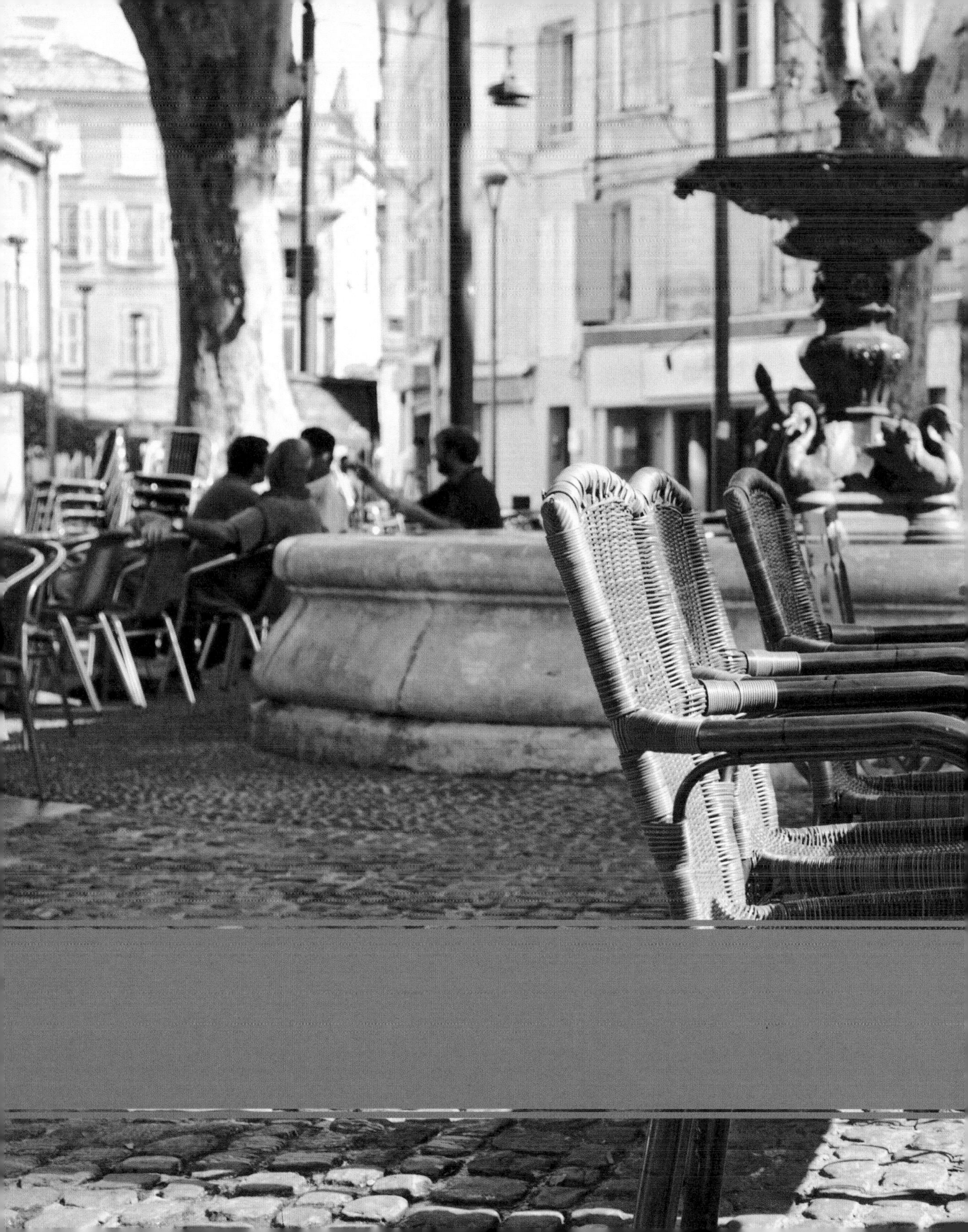

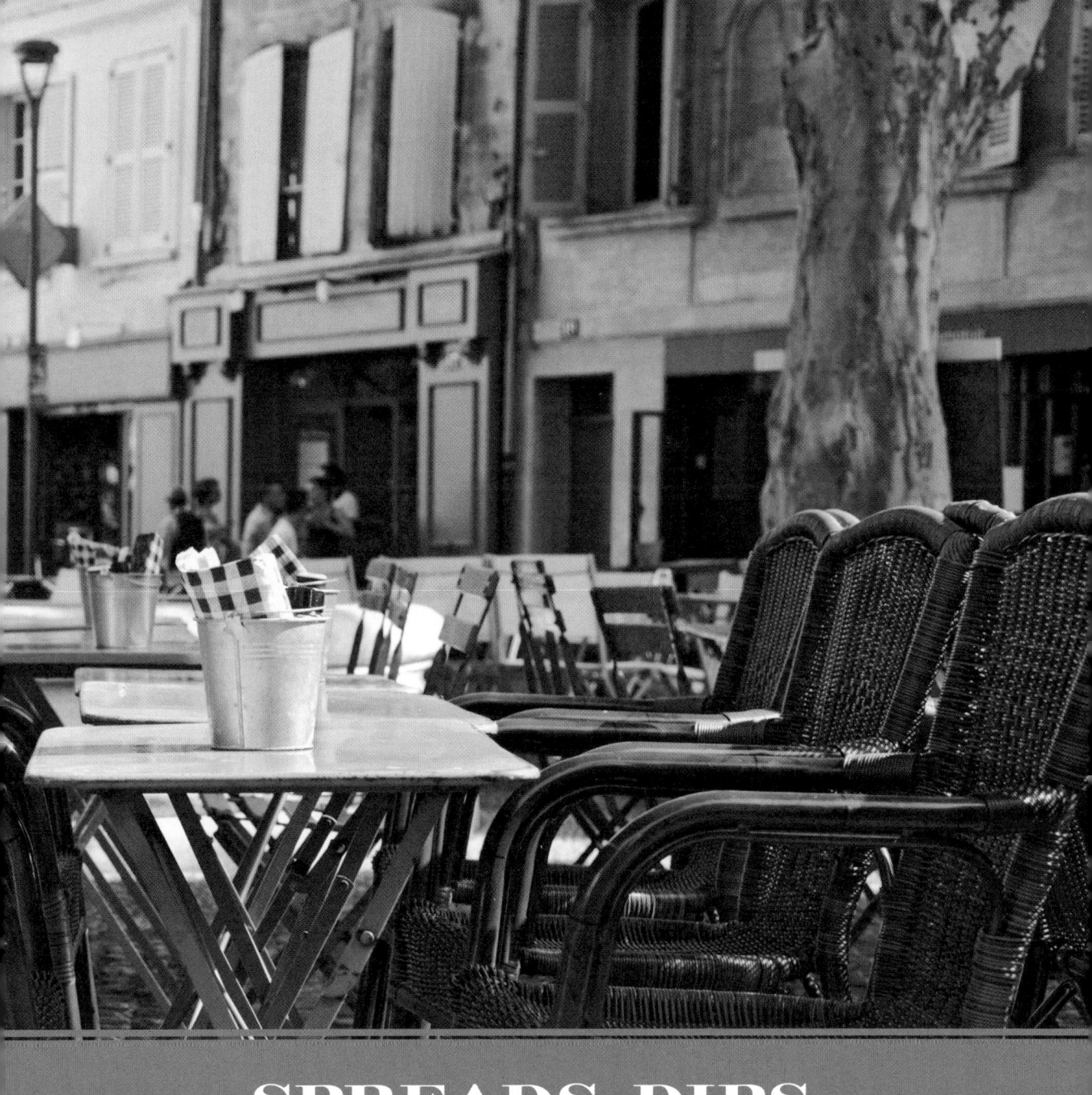

SPREADS, DIPS & APPETIZERS

BUTTERED GARLIC TOASTS WITH WHITE BEANS *and* CRISPY PORK

SERVES 6

These toasts hail from the Vendée region of west-central France, where the small, white Mogette bean has been grown for generations and is still used to make this traditional appetizer. In olden days, beans were simmered in pots set in or near the chimney; no doubt they were scooped from the pot and crushed directly onto toasts grilled in the same fireplace. The pork bits might have been trimmings from *jambon cru*, a local version of prosciutto that was once a feature of every French farmstead. The toasts can be prepared in the oven, but grilling adds that bit of smoky, charred flavor reminiscent of the chimney. This recipe makes about 20 small toasts.

4 tablespoons unsalted butter, plus more for spreading

½ of an onion, minced

½ pound Mogette de Vendée beans (or other small white beans, such as Alubia Blanca or Cannellini), picked over and soaked (see page 26)

1 teaspoon sea salt

½ teaspoon freshly ground black pepper

1 baguette or sweet bâtarde, cut into ½-inch diagonal slices

4 to 5 garlic cloves, peeled or unpeeled

3 ounces jambon cru or prosciutto, shredded, fried, and chopped

In a large saucepan over medium heat, melt the 4 tablespoons butter. When it foams, add the onion; sauté until translucent, about 2 minutes. Drain beans, reserving their soaking liquid, then add them to the pan, stirring for a few minutes. Add enough reserved liquid to cover beans by about 3 inches, and bring to a boil. Reduce heat to low; cover and cook for 30 minutes. Add salt and pepper; continue to cook until beans are tender, about another hour. Taste and adjust seasoning, as desired.

Prepare a grill: Build a wood or charcoal fire, preheat a gas grill, or place a stove-top grill pan over medium-high heat. Grill bread about 2 minutes per side or until slightly dry. Rub one side of each toast with garlic, then spread with remaining butter.

Drain beans and pile some on each toast, mashing with a fork. Sprinkle with a little crispy prosciutto and serve immediately.

Alternatively, let your guests prepare their own canapés: Set the table with the drained beans, a bowl of garlic cloves, another of prosciutto, a platter of grilled toasts, and a plate of butter. It's quite convivial!

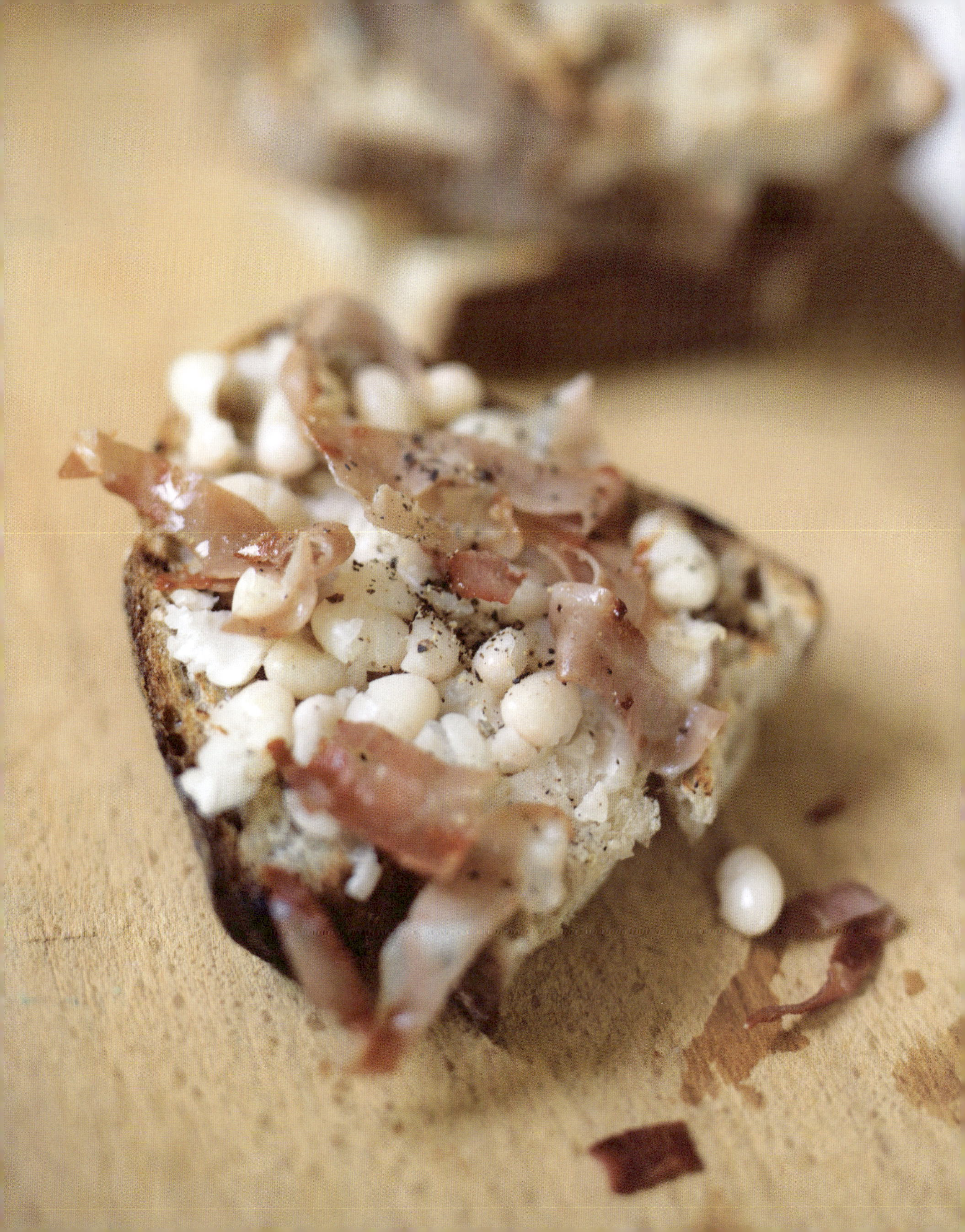

BLACK BEAN HUMMUS

SERVES 4

The French, like so many other cultures, are fans of hummus, that ubiquitous Middle Eastern dip of chickpeas, olive oil, and sesame paste. Variations — like this one using *haricots noirs*, or black beans — are popular at aperitif time, served along with toasts, crackers, or vegetable sticks. Tahini tends to separate in the jar, so stir it well before measuring. This recipe will yield about 2 cups; it can easily be scaled up if you are serving a crowd.

2 tablespoons tahini

2 garlic cloves, crushed and chopped

2 tablespoons extra-virgin olive oil, plus more for serving

2 cups cooked black beans (see page 26), with broth

Juice of ½ lemon

¼ to ½ teaspoon sea salt

In the bowl of a food processor, combine tahini, garlic, and olive oil; pulse a few times to mix. Drain beans, reserving broth. Add drained beans, lemon juice, and salt to the bowl; process until smooth. If the mixture is too thick, add a tablespoon or two of reserved bean broth and process again.

To serve, scrape the hummus into a bowl and drizzle with a little more olive oil.

GREEN LENTIL *and* GOAT CHEESE SPREAD WITH CHIVES

SERVES 4

Lentils are quite popular in France and are used in a variety of ways. Here, they're combined with tangy goat cheese and chives to make a simple spread for toasts, crackers, or sliced vegetables, such as cucumbers or black radishes. This recipe will yield 2½ to 3 cups.

½ cup green French lentils, picked over and rinsed

½ of a carrot

½ of a celery stalk

¼ of an onion

1 bay leaf

¼ to ½ teaspoon sea salt

2½ to 3 ounces soft goat cheese, at room temperature

1 tablespoon minced fresh chives, plus more for garnish

2 to 3 tablespoons heavy cream

¼ teaspoon Dijon mustard

Toasted baguette slices (optional)

In a saucepan over medium-high heat, add the lentils, carrot, celery, onion, and bay leaf, plus enough water to cover lentils by about 2 inches. Bring to a boil, then reduce heat to low. Add the salt; partially cover and cook for 20 to 30 minutes or until the lentils are tender to the bite. Do not overcook; a little texture is desirable.

Remove and discard the vegetables and bay leaf. Drain lentils and transfer to a bowl; let cool to room temperature.

Cut goat cheese into three or four pieces; add to the lentils along with the chives and half of the cream. Gently mix with a fork, mashing some of the lentils. Add the remaining cream and the mustard; continue to mix to achieve a spreadable consistency.

To serve, spread toasts with lentil mixture and garnish with chives. Alternatively, serve garnished lentil mixture in a bowl, with toasts on the side.

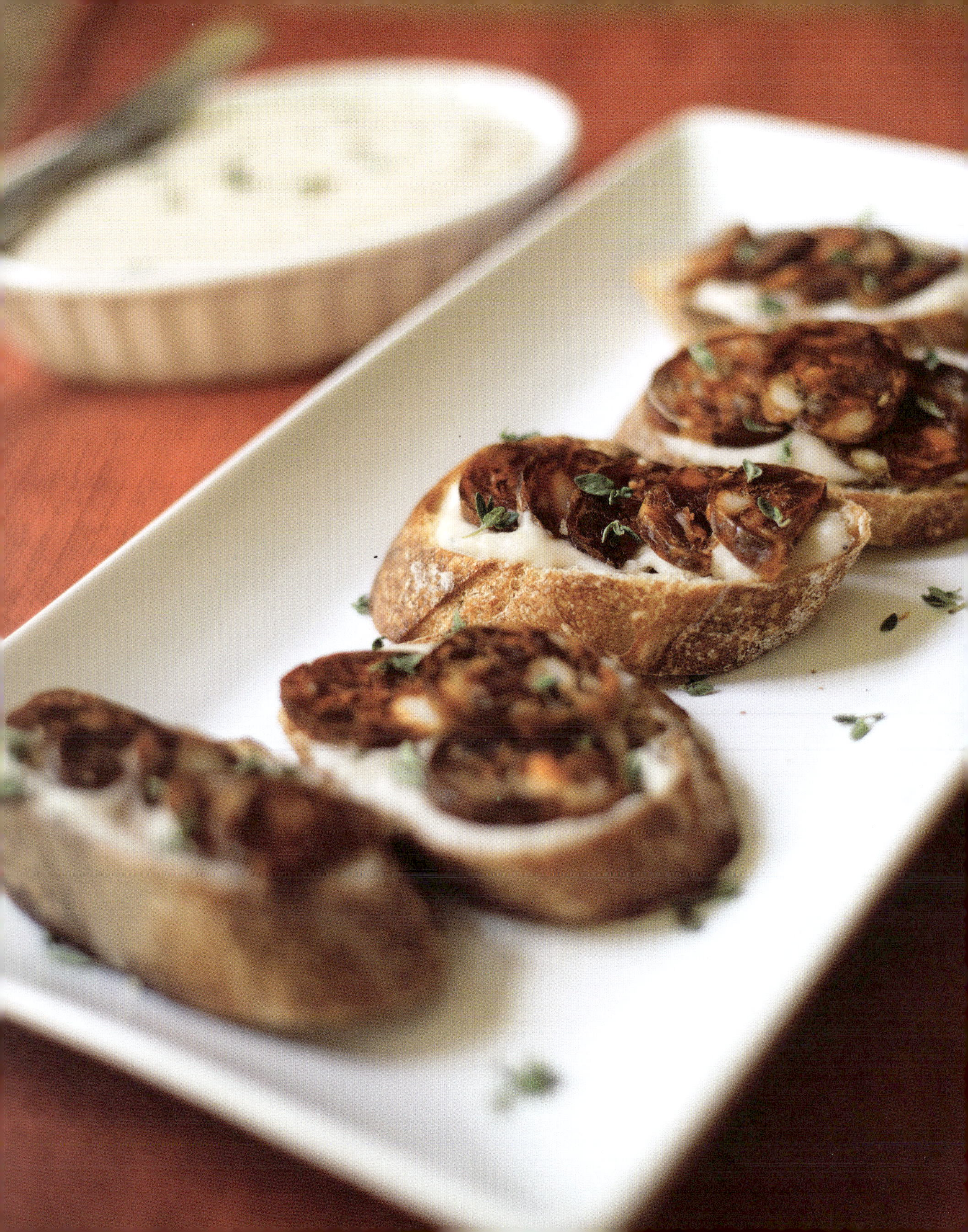

WHITE BEAN *and* CHORIZO TARTINES

SERVES 4

The French include chorizo — spicy dried sausage from neighboring Spain — on charcuterie platters and incorporate it into soups and stews. Spreading toasts with puréed white beans seasoned with fresh thyme and garnished with chorizo makes an interesting and contemporary appetizer.

1 cup cooked white beans, such as Lingot, Cannellini, Tarbais, Cassoulet, or Royal Corona (see page 26), drained

1 garlic clove, crushed and minced

½ teaspoon fresh thyme leaves, chopped, plus more for garnish

1 tablespoon heavy cream

1 teaspoon extra-virgin olive oil, plus more for toasts

¼ to ½ teaspoon sea salt

12 baguette slices

¼ pound dry, Spanish-style chorizo, cut into thin slices, then halved or quartered

Preheat oven to 400°F.

In a blender, purée beans, garlic, thyme, cream, olive oil, and ¼ teaspoon salt to make a smooth, spreadable paste. If the mixture is too thick, add a little more olive oil. Taste and adjust seasoning, as desired. Set aside.

On a baking sheet, arrange baguette slices and drizzle with a little olive oil. Place in the preheated oven and bake until light golden, about 10 minutes. Turn and toast the other side, another 5 minutes.

Spread toasts with bean mixture; garnish with several pieces of chorizo and a sprinkle of thyme.

FRIED PANISSE BATONS

SERVES 4 TO 6

Panisse is a traditional Provençal dish made with chickpea flour. Like polenta, it's cooked with water and olive oil, and stirred until it's very thick. The cooked mass is then spread onto a rimmed baking sheet or rolled in a towel, chilled until firm, and cut into sticks the size of thick French fries, or, if towel-wrapped, into thick rounds. When frying, aim for a crispy, golden crust with a creamy, soft interior. *Panisse* can be served as an appetizer or used as a side dish, much as you would fried polenta. This recipe makes about 20 pieces, depending on size and shape.

2 cups chickpea flour, sifted

1 quart hot water

1 tablespoon extra-virgin olive oil, plus a little for oiling the baking sheet, and more for frying

Coarse sea salt and freshly ground black pepper

In a large saucepan over medium-high heat, combine chickpea flour, water, and olive oil. Cook, whisking continuously, until the mixture thickens and starts to bubble, 2 to 3 minutes. Beat with a wooden spoon, stirring continuously until the mixture is very thick and heavy.

On an oiled baking sheet, spread the mixture in a scant ½-inch layer. Cover with plastic wrap and refrigerate at least 2 hours or overnight.

When ready to cook, cut the cooled mixture into 3- by ½-inch sticks. In a deep skillet or Dutch oven over medium-high heat, warm the oil to 375°F. (If you don't have a frying thermometer, test the temperature by adding a small piece of dough to the oil. If it begins to fry quickly, the oil is ready.) Fry the rectangles in small batches, turning to cook all sides until golden, about 1 minute per side. Remove to a paper towel–lined platter, and sprinkle with salt and pepper. Serve warm.

SPICY ROASTED CHICKPEAS

SERVES 4

For centuries, chickpeas have been cultivated throughout the Mediterranean region, including southern France, where they are still produced today. There are even chickpea festivals in some villages to celebrate the humble legume. Feel free to use different spices here. The trick is to make sure the chickpeas are well dried before seasoning them so they get crisp in the oven.

2 cups cooked chickpeas (see page 26), drained

2 teaspoons extra-virgin olive oil

½ teaspoon cumin seeds

½ teaspoon coriander seeds

¼ to ½ teaspoon chili powder, depending on the spiciness you want

Coarse sea salt and freshly ground black pepper

Preheat oven to 425°F.

Place drained chickpeas between 2 layers of paper towels; pat dry. Some of the skins may come off. You can discard these or keep them; they will roast up, too.

In a bowl, combine chickpeas, olive oil, cumin seeds, coriander seeds, and chili powder; stir well. On a baking sheet, spread spiced beans in a single layer; place in the preheated oven.

Roast until chickpeas begin to lightly brown and some split, 15 to 20 minutes. Taste; if you want them crispier, cook another 5 to 10 minutes, but be careful not to burn.

Remove to a bowl, sprinkle with salt and pepper, and serve hot or warm.

CREAMY WHITE BEAN and ANCHOVY DIP

MAKES ABOUT 1 CUP

Crème d'anchois is a favorite spread in France, especially in Provence. Because of the addition of crème fraîche or cream, it's a little less assertive than its better-known cousin *anchoïade*, which uses just garlic, anchovies, and olive oil. This recipe adds some white beans, too, which thickens the spread and mellows it even more. Serve with toasted bread slices or crudités.

1 cup cooked white beans, such as Lingot, Cannellini, Alubia Blanca, or Royal Corona (see page 26), drained

2 garlic cloves, crushed and minced

½ teaspoon fresh thyme

12 anchovy fillets, chopped

2 to 3 tablespoons heavy cream or crème fraîche

¼ to ½ teaspoon sea salt

In a blender, combine beans, garlic, thyme, anchovies, 1 tablespoon cream, and ¼ teaspoon salt. Purée, gradually adding more cream as needed to achieve a smooth, spreadable consistency. Taste and adjust seasoning as needed.

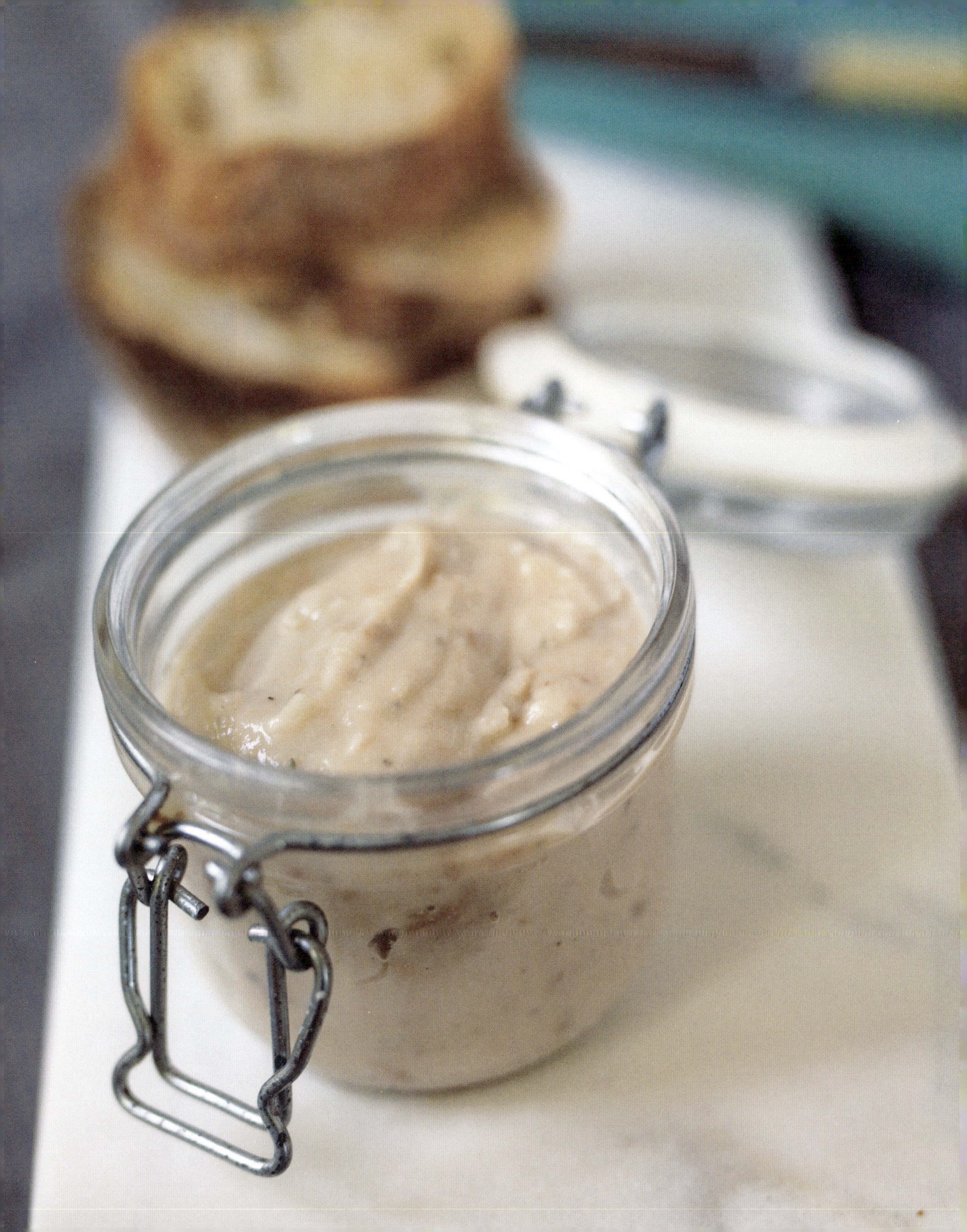

SMOKED SALMON *and* WHITE BEAN RILLETTES

MAKES 1½ CUPS

A common offering at aperitif time, rillettes are made with shredded meat — pork, poultry, rabbit, duck, or fish — creamed with fat and seasonings to make a smooth paste for spreading on breads or crackers. This version combines two types of salmon for extra flavor, and adds silky Cannellini beans for texture. It's rounded out with both butter and mayonnaise, and seasoned with dill and shallots.

2 tablespoons unsalted butter, at room temperature

1½ cups cooked white beans, such as Lingot, Cannellini, or Alubia Blanca (see page 26), drained

2 green onions, white parts only, minced

2 tablespoons minced shallot

1 tablespoon minced fresh dill

½ to 1 teaspoon lemon juice

⅓ cup mayonnaise

4 ounces hot-smoked salmon

2 ounces gravlax or other cured salmon, minced

Sea salt and freshly ground black pepper

In a bowl, combine butter, beans, green onions, shallot, dill, and lemon juice. Using a wooden spoon or an electric mixer, mash and stir until creamy. Mix in mayonnaise. Crumble hot-smoked salmon into the mixture, stirring until fully blended into a spreadable paste. Fold in cured salmon. Taste and add salt and pepper; adjust seasoning, as desired. Pack tightly into a jar or bowl. Cover and refrigerate overnight, or up to three days.

Serve slightly chilled.

HARICOTS DE SOISSONS
with MAROILLES CHEESE

SERVES 4 TO 6

This appetizer — combining large, whole beans with small cubes of strong cheese — seemed a bit odd to me, but once I tried it, I became a fan. Both Soissons beans and Maroilles cheese come from northern France, and both are similarly difficult to find outside of France. My version uses Royal Corona beans and Munster cheese, which is milder than Maroilles. If you'd like to use a stronger cheese, try Port Salut, which is similar in texture to Maroilles.

2 cups cooked Royal Corona or Soissons beans (see page 26), drained

½ pound Munster or Maroilles cheese, cut in ½-inch cubes

1 to 2 tablespoons extra-virgin olive oil

¼ teaspoon coarse sea salt

½ teaspoon freshly ground black pepper

On a platter or four salad plates, place beans in one layer and tuck the cubed cheese among the beans. Drizzle with olive oil, and sprinkle with salt and pepper. Serve at room temperature.

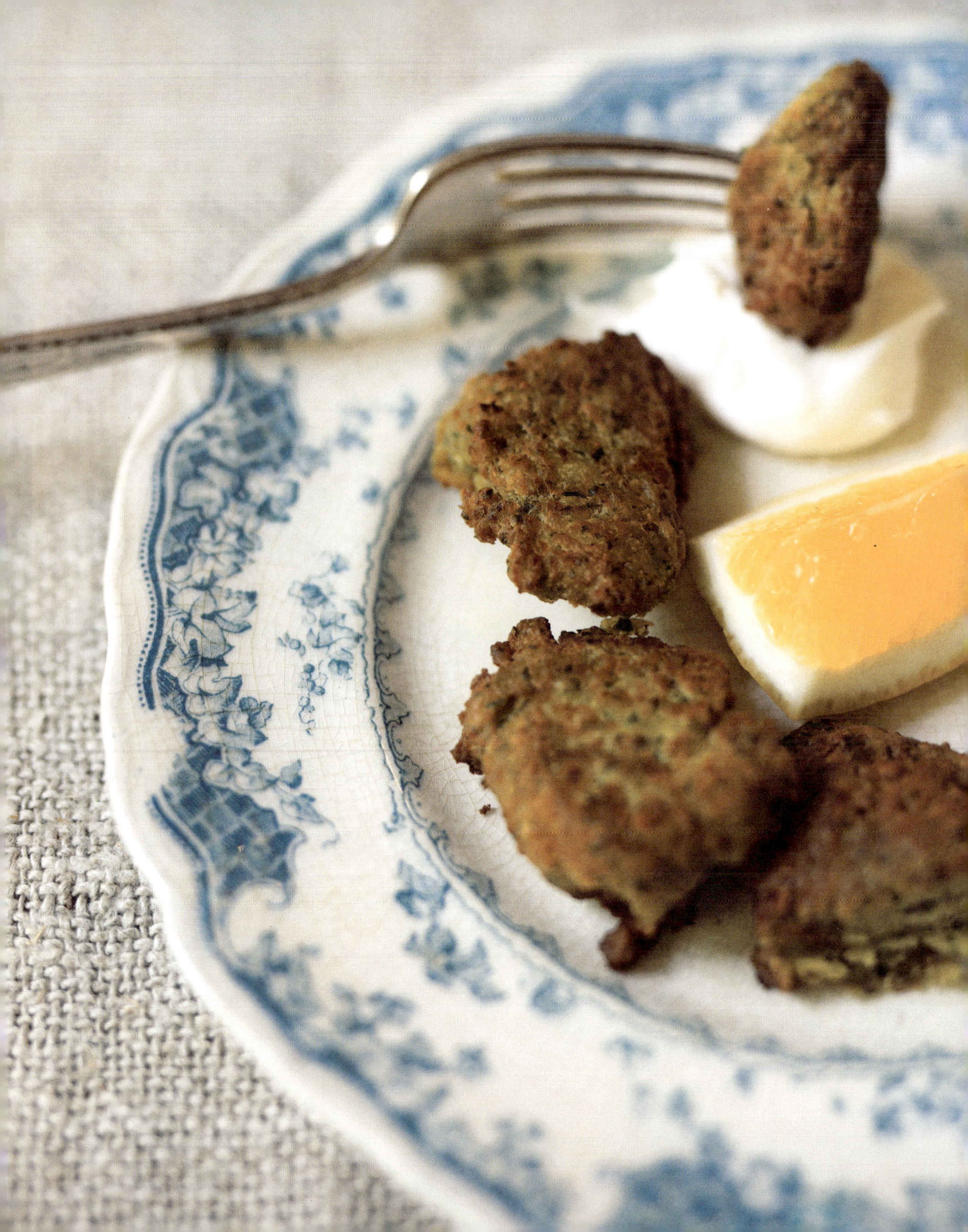

CHICKPEA BEIGNETS

SERVES 4

The French are fond of all sorts of hot, savory fritters at aperitif time. When made spoon-size and served with lemons, these beignets resemble the salt-cod fritters of the French West Indies known as *accra*, but they also feature some of the same ingredients as Middle Eastern falafel. This recipe will make about 30 spoon-size fritters, 24 small patties, or 12 larger patties.

2 cups cooked chickpeas (see page 26), drained

¼ cup finely chopped flat-leaf parsley

¼ cup finely chopped cilantro

3 garlic cloves, crushed and finely chopped

1 teaspoon ground cumin

¼ teaspoon cayenne pepper

¼ teaspoon red pepper flakes

Juice of ½ lemon, plus 3 lemons cut into quarters for serving

¼ to ½ teaspoon sea salt

¼ teaspoon freshly ground black pepper

1 egg

2 to 3 tablespoons all-purpose flour

Extra-virgin olive oil, for frying

½ to 1 cup crème fraîche (optional)

In the bowl of a food processor, combine chickpeas, parsley, cilantro, garlic, cumin, cayenne, pepper flakes, lemon juice, ¼ teaspoon salt, pepper, and egg; process into a thick paste. Add 2 tablespoons flour; process into a stiff dough that can be shaped into a patty. If the batter is too sticky, add another tablespoon of flour. Taste and adjust seasoning, as desired.

In a large skillet, add olive oil to a depth of ⅓ inch; warm over medium-high heat to 350 to 375°F. (If you don't have a frying thermometer, test the temperature by adding a small piece of dough to the oil. If it begins to fry quickly, the oil is ready.) Make irregular, bite-size beignets: Use a tablespoon to scoop bits of dough, and carefully push them off the spoon into the hot oil. Repeat, leaving about an inch between beignets in the pan. Turn beignets once or twice, frying until golden brown. Remove with a slotted spoon to a paper towel–lined plate; repeat until all batter is used.

Alternatively, using your hands, shape patties between 1 and 2 inches in diameter and about ⅓-inch thick. Slide patties into the hot oil and cook as above.

Serve hot, accompanied by lemon quarters and crème fraîche, if desired.

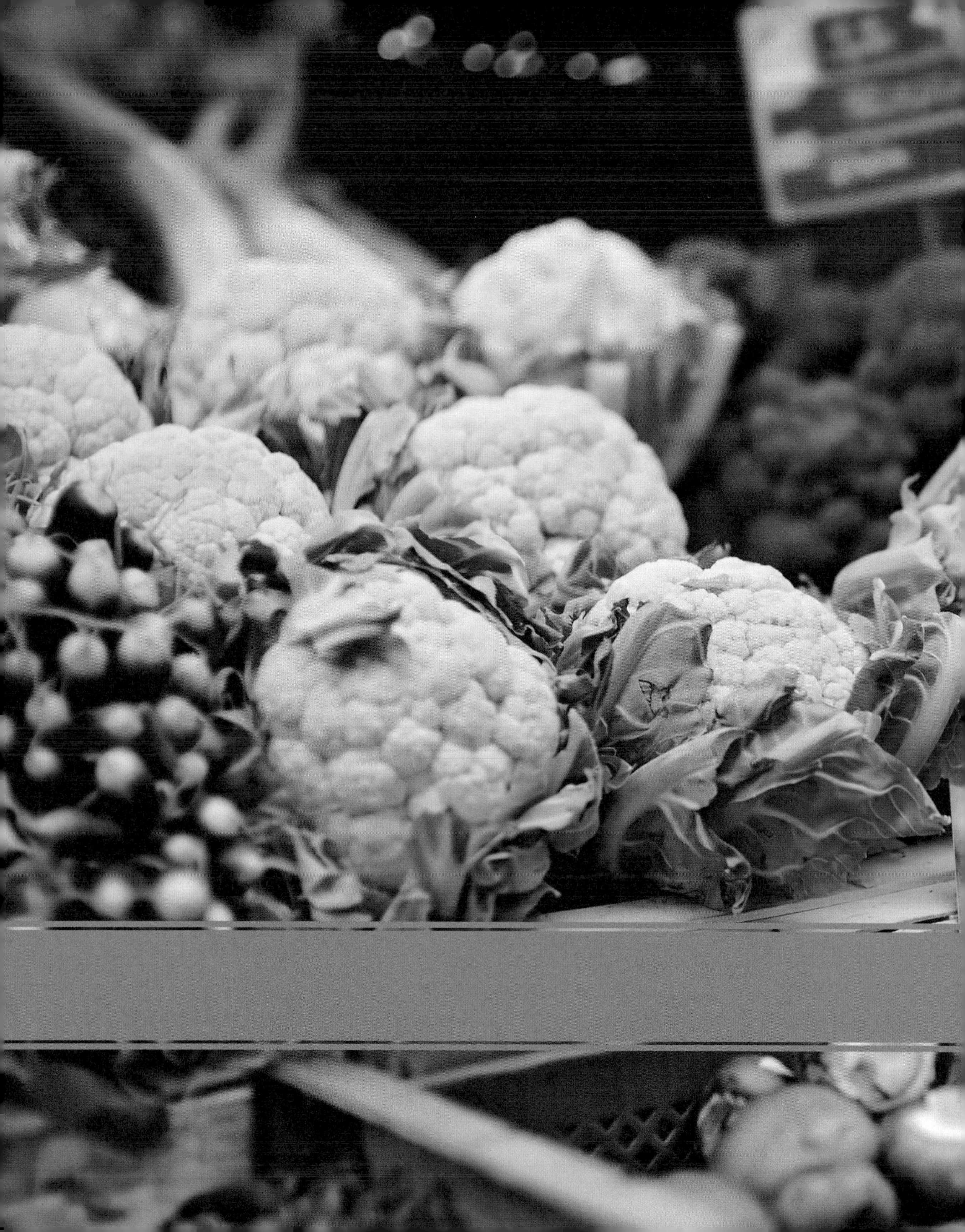

SALADS

SALADE NIÇOISE WITH SEARED TUNA AND WHITE BEANS
PAGE 51

SALADE NIÇOISE: *from* SIMPLE SOUTHERN MEAL TO *International* FAVORITE

Like many of the dishes of Provence and the Mediterranean coast, Salade Niçoise was once poor people's food. People used what they had grown, caught, produced, or preserved themselves. The original version of the salad, which probably dates from the 19th century, was most likely tomatoes, eggs, and anchovies — all abundant in the Mediterranean — plus olive oil. Jacques Médecin, the former mayor of Nice, and author of the definitive *La Cuisine du Comté de Nice* (Julliard, 1972), which I bought shortly after it first appeared and still treasure, insists that no cooked vegetables be used, only raw. No boiled potatoes or green beans for him. Tomatoes, olives, fresh fava beans, hard-boiled eggs, either oil-packed tuna or anchovies — never both — and no vinegar: just olive oil, salt, and pepper.

Another authority on the food of Provence, Jean-Noël Escudier, author of *The Wonderful Food of Provence* (Houghton-Mifflin, 1968), provides us with his classic version: Tomatoes, anchovies, perhaps some olive oil–packed tuna, green bell peppers, and black olives, sprinkled with olive oil and vinegar plus a little black pepper. Sliced eggs and basil leaves are an optional garnish. The ingredients are to be composed on a round or oval platter, not tossed in a salad bowl.

Both of these versions are far simpler than what you'd get in a restaurant in today's Nice — or anywhere else around the world — where boiled potatoes and green beans appear side by side with tuna and anchovies, sometimes with beets, fennel, cucumber, artichokes, seasonal white beans instead of green, as well as the traditional tomatoes, olives, and eggs, and perhaps a scattering of capers. A vinaigrette finishes the modern salad, which may or may not include lettuce.

Perhaps the biggest departure from the classic is the now-common version made with seared fresh tuna, thinly sliced or served as a steak, surrounded by the vegetables. Monsieur Médecin would have been horrified.

The key thing about Salade Niçoise, no matter how lush or austere, is to use only the best ingredients. It is better to omit the green beans if they are not crisp and fresh, and to use cherry tomatoes if summer-ripe tomatoes are not in season. Using farm-fresh eggs with golden yolks, fruity extra-virgin olive oil, and a good wine vinegar or fresh lemon juice will make a difference in the quality of your salad.

SALADE NIÇOISE *with* CRANBERRY BEANS *and* TUNA CONFIT

SERVES 4

It is quite easy to make your own tuna confit. Slowly cooked in olive oil, the fish achieves a velvety texture, which pairs well with meaty Cranberry beans and makes for a fancy, restaurant-quality dish. You can also use tuna confit in any recipe that calls for jarred tuna packed in olive oil.

FOR THE TUNA

- ¾ to 1 pound fresh sushi-grade ahi tuna, about 2 inches thick
- ½ to 1 teaspoon sea salt
- ½ teaspoon freshly ground black pepper
- ½ to 1 cup extra-virgin olive
- 1 bay leaf

FOR THE BEANS

- 1 to 2 tablespoons lemon juice
- ¼ teaspoon sea salt
- ¼ teaspoon freshly ground black pepper
- 1 tablespoon chopped flat-leaf parsley (divided use)
- 3 cups cooked Cranberry beans (see page 26), warmed in their broth

TO FINISH

- 4 large, ripe tomatoes, quartered lengthwise, or 12 to 16 cherry tomatoes, halved
- 1 green bell pepper, stemmed, seeded, and stemmed, sliced lengthwise into thin strips
- ¼ cup black olives, any kind
- 1½ tablespoons capers, rinsed and drained

Season tuna all over with salt and pepper; set aside. In a small saucepan, add olive oil to a generous ½-inch depth. Add bay leaf; warm oil over medium-high heat, then reduce heat to medium. Using tongs, gently lower fish into oil. Watch as fish becomes opaque from the bottom up. When it is opaque up to the ½- to ¾-inch level (about 3 to 4 minutes), gently turn it, using tongs and a spatula if necessary, and repeat the other side. Remove fish when about ½ inch of the midsection is still pink. Set aside, reserving the olive oil.

In a bowl large enough to hold the beans, combine 3 tablespoons of the olive oil used to poach the fish and the lemon juice. Add salt and pepper; mix well with a fork. Taste and adjust seasoning, as desired, and add half the parsley.

Drain beans and put them in the bowl with the oil-and-lemon mixture; fold gently. Taste and adjust seasoning again.

Arrange beans on 4 dinner plates or shallow bowls. Top each serving with one-quarter of the poached tuna; garnish with tomatoes, green peppers, and black olives. Finish with a sprinkle of capers and the reserved parsley.

SALADE NIÇOISE *with* SEARED TUNA *and* WHITE BEANS

SERVES 4

This personal favorite of mine nods to Nice's proximity to the Italian border. Nice didn't become a part of modern France until 1860, and maintains strong culinary roots in the country where tuna-and-bean salads are a tradition. The beans are dressed separately before joining the rest of the ingredients on the plate, which gives them their own identity.

FOR THE BEANS

3 tablespoons extra-virgin olive oil

1 teaspoon red wine vinegar

¼ teaspoon sea salt

¼ teaspoon freshly ground black pepper

1½ tablespoons minced flat-leaf parsley

3 cups cooked white beans (see page 26), such as Coco Blanc, Lingot, Tarbais, Cassoulet, or Cannellini, drained

FOR THE VINAIGRETTE

⅓ cup extra-virgin olive oil

1 to 2 tablespoons lemon juice

2 teaspoons Dijon mustard

¼ teaspoon salt

2 tablespoons thinly sliced basil leaves

TO FINISH

¾ to 1 pound sushi-grade ahi tuna steak, about 1½ inches thick

¼ to ½ teaspoon sea salt

¼ to ½ teaspoon freshly ground black pepper

1 tablespoon extra-virgin olive oil

1 pound new potatoes, such as Yukon Gold or fingerling

1 pound haricots verts (or other thin green beans), stem ends trimmed

4 large, ripe tomatoes, quartered lengthwise, or 12 to 16 cherry tomatoes, halved

½ cup oil-cured Niçoise or other black olives

1 cucumber, thinly sliced

4 large hard-boiled eggs, peeled and quartered lengthwise

To prepare the beans: In a medium bowl, combine olive oil, red wine vinegar, salt, pepper, and parsley. Mix well with a fork. Add drained beans and gently fold with a spoon to coat. Set aside.

To make the vinaigrette: In a bowl, combine olive oil and lemon juice; mix well with a fork. Add mustard and salt; mix again until thickened. Stir in basil, and set aside.

To prepare the fish, season it on both sides with salt and pepper. In a skillet over high heat, warm the olive oil. When hot, add tuna. When the first quarter-inch turns opaque, turn and sear the other side; the interior of the steak should be red to pink. Remove tuna from pan and cut into thin slices.

In a saucepan over medium-high heat, add the potatoes and enough water to cover potatoes by about 2 inches. Bring water to a boil. Reduce heat to medium; cook until potatoes are easily pierced with the tip of a knife, 10 to 20 minutes, depending on size. Drain and set aside. Keep water simmering and add green beans, cooking until just tender, about 7 to 10 minutes. Drain.

When cool, cut potatoes in half or in quarters, depending upon their size.

Arrange marinated white beans on one side of the plate or platter, and follow with the rest of the components, fanning tuna slices in the center.

Stir the vinaigrette, then drizzle it over all.

CLASSIC SALADE NIÇOISE

SERVES 4

This is the most common version of Salade Niçoise found today in France. High summer is the ideal time for enjoying these flavors, but it is made and served year-round.

FOR THE VINAIGRETTE

⅓ cup extra-virgin olive oil

1 to 2 tablespoons red wine vinegar

2 teaspoons Dijon mustard

¼ teaspoon salt

FOR THE SALAD

1 pound red, white, or gold new potatoes

1 pound haricots verts (or other thin green beans), stem ends trimmed

1 small head butter lettuce, leaves separated

4 large hard-boiled eggs, peeled and quartered lengthwise

1 green bell pepper, seeded and stemmed, sliced lengthwise into thin strips

4 large, ripe tomatoes, quartered lengthwise, or 12 to 16 cherry tomatoes, halved

A 6-ounce jar of oil-packed tuna

12 anchovy fillets, oil-packed or salt-packed, rinsed and patted dry

½ cup oil-cured black olives, pitted if desired, or ½ cup Niçoise olives

2 tablespoons capers, rinsed and drained (optional)

½ teaspoon freshly ground black pepper

To make the vinaigrette: In a bowl, combine olive oil and vinegar to taste; mix well with a fork. Add mustard and salt; mix again until thickened. Set aside.

In a saucepan over medium-high heat, cover potatoes with water by 2 inches; bring to a boil. Reduce heat to medium; cook until potatoes are easily pierced with the tip of a knife, 10 to 20 minutes, depending on size. Using a slotted spoon, remove potatoes and set aside. Keep water simmering and add green beans, cooking until just tender, about 7 to 10 minutes. Drain.

When cool, cut potatoes in half or in quarters, depending upon their size.

On a platter or 4 dinner plates, arrange a layer of lettuce leaves. Top with potatoes, green beans, eggs, pepper, and tomatoes. Scatter with chunks of tuna and anchovy fillets, olives, and capers, if using. Season with black pepper and drizzle all over with vinaigrette.

Serve at room temperature.

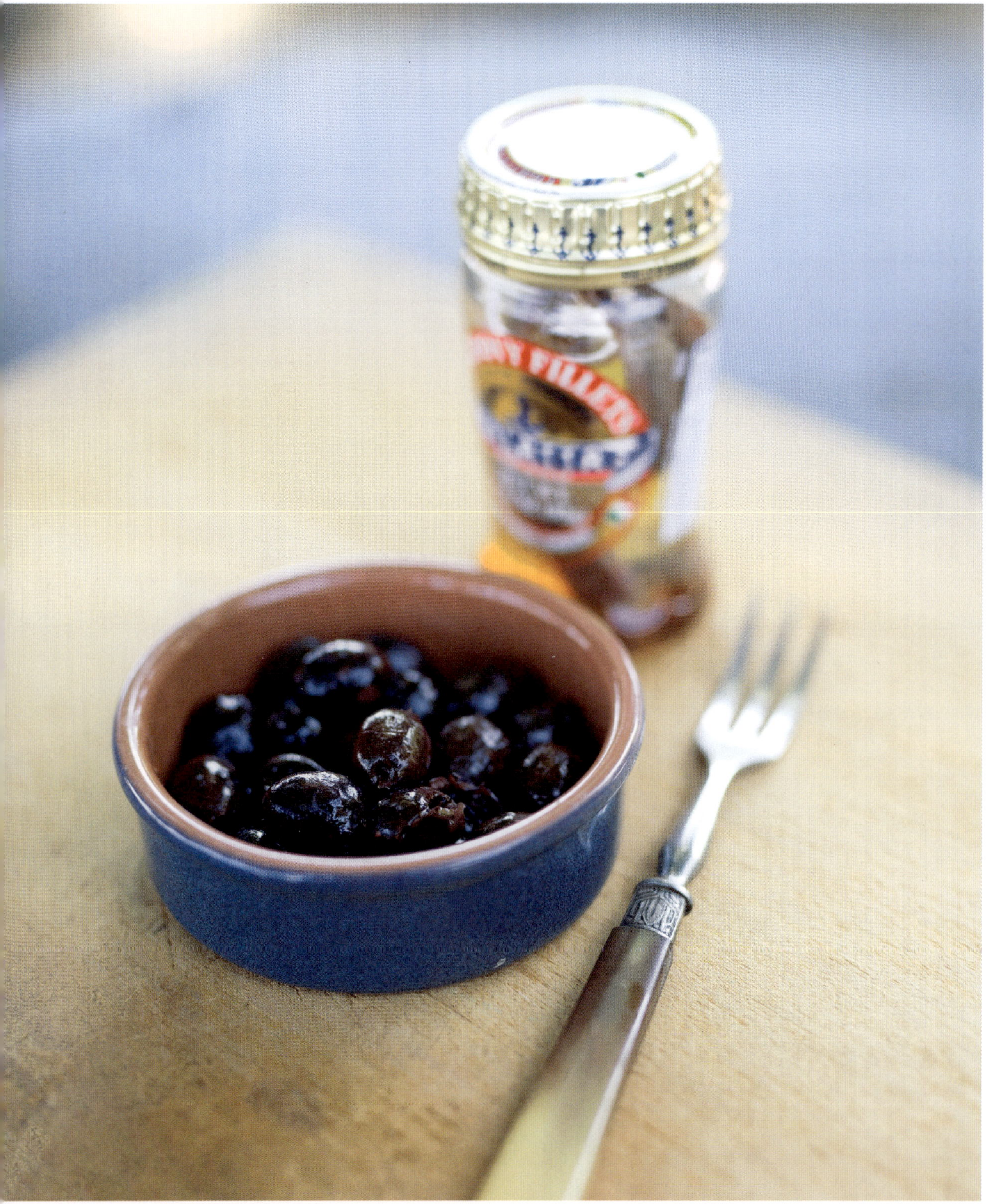

WHITE BEAN, WATERCRESS, *and* PICKLED HERRING SALAD

SERVES 4

By combining plump white beans with pickled herring and a little of its marinade, we turn a French bistro favorite into a special salad — perfect as a first course or as part of a small-plates buffet. Watercress leaves can be used as a bed for the other ingredients or, as they are here, combined with the beans and fish. Jars of pickled herring are readily found in supermarket aisles alongside refrigerated pickles and sauerkraut.

1 bunch watercress

4 cups cooked white beans, such as Lingot, Cannellini, Tarbais, or Cassoulet (see page 26), drained

6 to 8 ounces pickled herring in marinade (dill marinade is especially good)

¼ cup minced red onions

Remove leafy sprigs from half the watercress, and leaves from the other half, discarding stems or reserving them for another use. Set sprigs and leaves aside.

Divide beans evenly among 4 salad plates. Drain herring, reserving marinade. Cut herring into bite-size pieces, and divide equally among plated beans. Add some pickled onions from the marinade to the plates. Sprinkle plates equally with red onions, and drizzle with 1 to 2 teaspoons of reserved marinade. Garnish with watercress leaves and sprigs, tucking some in among beans and herring.

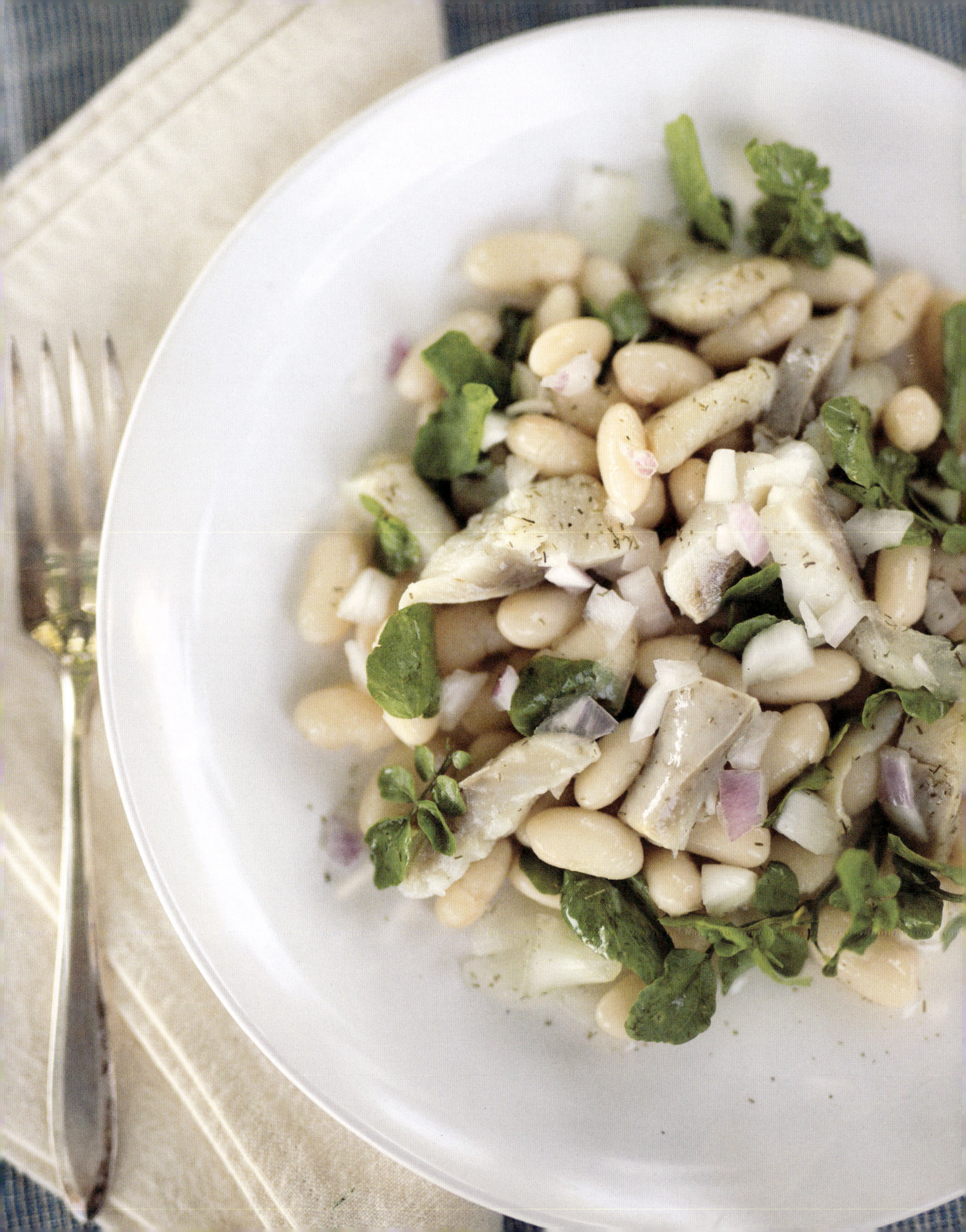

WHITE BEANS with LARDONS, RED PEPPERS, and PIMENT D'ESPELETTE

SERVES 4

Salty, sweet, and a little bit spicy, this salad harkens to the Basque Country where, in late summer and early fall, the stone facades of buildings of the village of Espelette turn bright red with hanging strands of drying peppers. This salad can be served on its own or to accompany grilled meats. *Lardons* are slab bacon sliced into 1- by ¼-inch matchsticks. French bacon is unsalted, so be mindful of additional salt if you use regular bacon.

1 large sweet red pepper

½ cup lardons, or 5 slices of thick bacon, cut into ¼-inch pieces

3 cups cooked small white beans, such as Alubia Blanca, Cannellini, or Coco Blanc (see page 26), drained and held at room temperature

2 tablespoons extra-virgin olive oil, as needed

¼ teaspoon sea salt

¼ to ½ teaspoon Piment d'Espelette (or ⅛ teaspoon cayenne pepper)

2 teaspoons red wine vinegar

½ cup wild arugula (optional)

Under a broiler (or on a stove-top grill), roast the red pepper until charred, turning often. Place pepper in a heavy paper bag and let stand at least 10 minutes and up to 30. Remove pepper and slip off charred skin. Cut pepper in half and remove ribs and seeds. Cut pepper lengthwise into thin strips. Set aside.

In a skillet over medium-high heat, fry *lardons* or bacon until crispy. Using a slotted spoon, remove meat to a bowl large enough to hold the beans. Reserve fat in the pan.

Reduce heat to medium and, using a slotted spoon, add half the beans to the pan. Gently stir to combine with bacon fat, then remove to the bowl with the *lardons*. Repeat with the remaining beans, adding a little olive oil if there is not enough fat.

To the bowl with the *lardons* and beans, add reserved roasted pepper strips, salt, Piment d'Espelette, and vinegar; gently fold to combine.

Serve in a shallow serving bowl or on individual plates. Garnish with wild arugula, if desired.

SALAD OF SALT COD and WHITE BEANS

SERVES 4

One of the traditional dishes of Provence is Brandade de Morue, a purée made with salt cod, garlic, olive oil, and potatoes, sprinkled with bread crumbs, and baked before being spread on grilled toasts. This salad captures the flavor of that combination, as beans take the place of potatoes. With these few, simple ingredients, you'll want to choose an assertive, flavorful olive oil. I like to serve this salad on a bed of wild arugula or shredded radicchio with grilled garlic toasts. The salt cod needs to be soaked for 24 hours before using, so plan ahead.

1 pound salt cod

3 tablespoons extra-virgin olive oil

1½ to 2 tablespoons red wine vinegar

2 garlic cloves, minced

½ to 1 teaspoon sea salt and freshly ground black pepper

3 cups cooked cooked Tarbais, Cassoulet, Lingot, or Coco Blanc beans (see page 26), drained

1 cup wild arugula or ½ cup shredded radicchio

Grilled garlic toasts (optional; see page 32)

In a large bowl, add salt cod and enough cold water to cover by about an inch. Refrigerate for at least 24 hours, changing water 3 or 4 times to refresh the fish and remove most of the salt.

In a skillet over medium-high heat, add enough water to come halfway up the sides of the pan; bring to just below a boil. Reduce heat to medium-low and gently poach soaked cod until it flakes easily with a fork, 10 to 15 minutes. With a slotted spoon or spatula, remove fish to a plate. Remove and discard any pieces of skin. Flake the fish, discarding any bones.

In a large bowl, combine olive oil, vinegar, garlic, salt, and pepper. Mix well with a fork. Add beans and flaked fish; gently fold to coat well.

Line a salad bowl or serving platter with arugula or radicchio, and top with dressed bean-and-fish mixture; sprinkle with more pepper, and serve with garlic toasts, if desired.

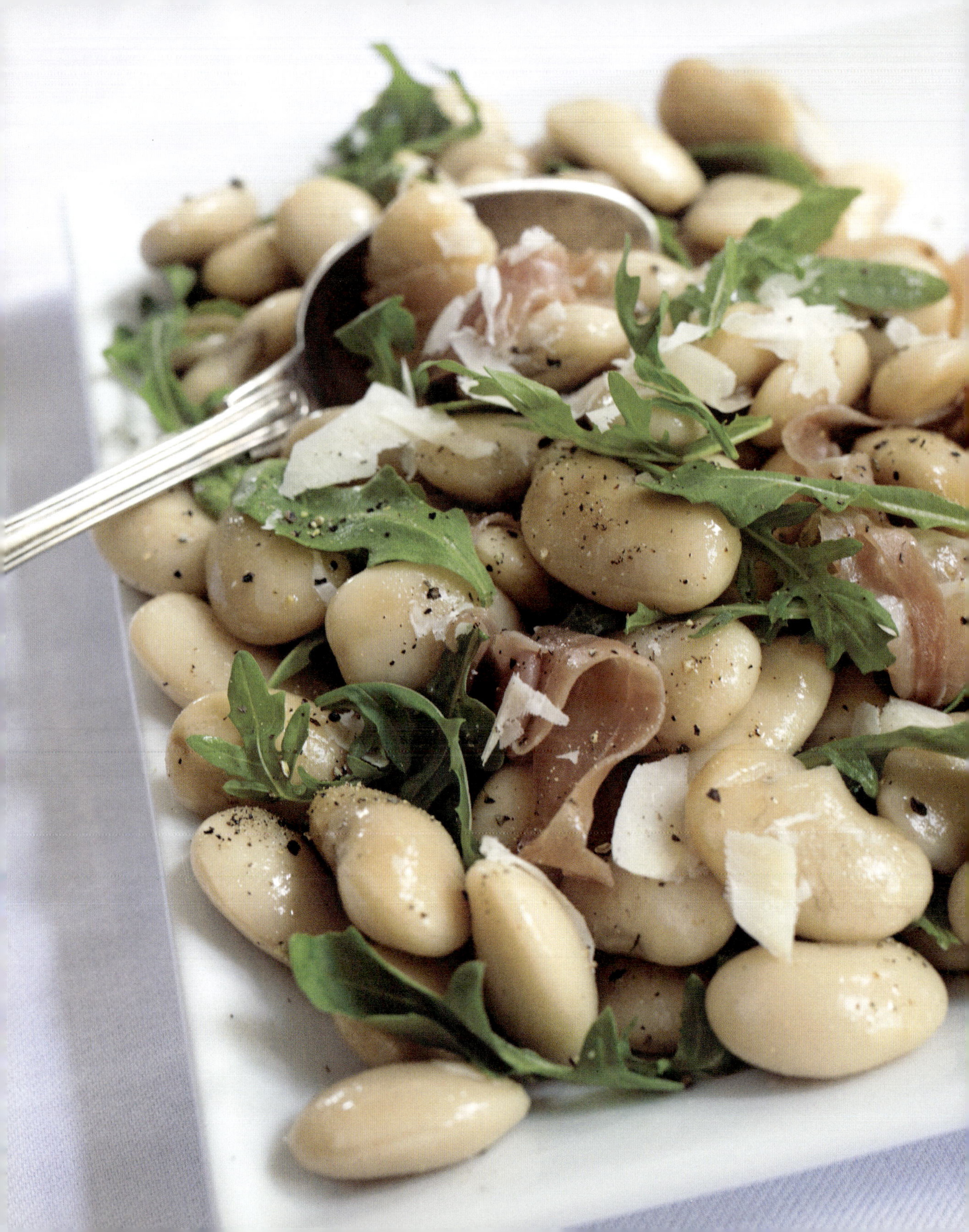

WHITE BEANS *with* ARUGULA, PROSCIUTTO, *and* PARMESAN VINAIGRETTE

SERVES 4 TO 6

The kind of salad that might be found at a *traiteur* (delicatessen) in France, this makes an excellent choice for a picnic or other casual affair. Large, meaty Soissons beans are typical for this simple salad, but Royal Coronas or other large beans work just as well.

2 ounces freshly grated Parmesan cheese (about ½ cup), plus more for garnish

5 tablespoons extra-virgin olive oil

2 teaspoons red wine vinegar

4 cups cooked Soissons, Royal Corona, or other large, meaty white bean (see page 26), drained

6 thin slices prosciutto, cut into 1-inch strips

2 cups baby arugula or wild arugula (divided use)

¼ teaspoon freshly ground black pepper

In a small bowl, whisk together cheese, oil, and vinegar until thick and creamy.

In a large, shallow serving bowl, combine beans, prosciutto, and most of the arugula; add the dressing and fold gently to coat. Garnish with remaining arugula, plus black pepper and more Parmesan cheese.

DUCK BREAST, LENTIL, *and* GREEN HERB SALAD

SERVES 4

In France, you can easily buy cured, sliced duck breast, ready to use, which is perfect for this main-dish bean salad featuring green French lentils. Here, I've seared and thinly sliced fresh duck breast, which creates a slightly different version of the salad — a little richer, but equally good. The tangy vinaigrette, made with Dijon mustard and pistachio oil, complements the duck and elevates the modest lentils.

½ pound green French lentils, picked over and rinsed

1½ teaspoons sea salt (divided use)

4 tablespoons pistachio oil

1 teaspoon Dijon mustard

1 tablespoon sherry vinegar

2 tablespoons minced shallot

1 tablespoon minced flat-leaf parsley, plus 4 sprigs for garnish

1 tablespoon minced chives

½ teaspoon freshly ground black pepper (divided use)

1- to 1¼-pound skin-on duck breast, at room temperature

1 tablespoon unsalted butter, at room temperature

1 teaspoon minced tarragon

In a saucepan over medium-high heat, add lentils plus enough water to cover by about 2 inches. Bring to a boil, then reduce heat to low. Add ½ teaspoon salt; partially cover and cook until the lentils are tender to the bite, 20 to 30 minutes. Drain and set aside.

In a large bowl, combine pistachio oil, mustard, vinegar, shallot, minced parsley, chives, ¼ teaspoon salt, and ¼ teaspoon pepper; whisk into a vinaigrette. Add lentils and gently toss; set aside.

Using a sharp knife, cut a crosshatch pattern through the skin of the duck breast and into the fat — but not into the meat — allowing about ½ inch between cuts. Pat meat dry and season both sides well with remaining salt and pepper.

Spread butter in a cool skillet. Place duck breasts in the skillet, skin-side down, then place the pan over medium heat. (Slow cooking in the unheated pan will allow the fat between the skin and the meat to render, while creating the crisp skin you're looking for.) Continue to cook until skin is crisp and golden, about 7 to 8 minutes for large, thick breasts.

Turn duck breasts and sear the other side, cooking until skin is browned and meat is cooked medium to medium-rare, 4 to 6 minutes. Using tongs, turn and hold the breasts to sear the sides as well.

Remove meat to a clean cutting board; let stand for 5 minutes before carving into ½-inch slices.

To serve, divide lentils among four plates and arrange duck slices on top. Drizzle with cutting board juices, if desired, and garnish with minced tarragon and parsley sprigs.

SMOKED TROUT, CELERY, and WHITE BEANS with TARRAGON VINAIGRETTE

SERVES 4

Creamy white beans combined with flaky bits of fish and crunchy celery makes an appetizing first course or small plate. Tarragon, one of the classic *fines herbes*, doubles its flavor here, first in the vinaigrette and again as an integral ingredient.

2 teaspoons Dijon mustard

2 teaspoons Champagne vinegar

¼ teaspoon sea salt

⅛ teaspoon freshly ground black pepper

1 tablespoon chopped fresh tarragon

3 tablespoons extra-virgin olive oil

1 tablespoon walnut oil

4 celery stalks

6 ounces smoked trout

2 cups cooked Lingot, Cannellini, Tarbais, or Cassoulet beans (see page 26), drained

2 tablespoons fresh tarragon leaves

To make the vinaigrette, combine mustard, vinegar, salt, pepper, and chopped tarragon in a bowl. Add olive oil and walnut oil; mix well with a fork or whisk to make a thick dressing. Set aside.

Trim celery stalks and thinly slice, using a mandoline if possible. Set aside.

Remove skin from the trout and flake into medium pieces.

Divide beans, celery, and trout among 4 salad plates, tucking some celery slices and fish into the beans. Drizzle with vinaigrette, and garnish with tarragon leaves. Serve at room temperature.

SALADE MEXICAINE

SERVES 4 TO 6

This is a French interpretation of a Mexican-style salad using beans, corn, and sweet red peppers. For many years, the French disdained corn as food fit only for animals, but the popularity of international dishes such as Chili con Carne and Salade Mexicaine has led to the growing availability of corn, black beans, and Kidney beans in supermarkets. Canned or frozen corn kernels are typically used in this French take on a Mexican salad. Fresh sweet corn is still rare in France, but feel free to use it in this recipe when it's in season.

Juice of 1 lime (about 2 teaspoons)

3 tablespoons extra-virgin olive oil

2 teaspoons Dijon mustard

½ teaspoon paprika

¼ teaspoon sea salt

¼ teaspoon freshly ground black pepper

4 cups cooked black beans or Kidney beans (see page 26), drained

2 cups thawed frozen corn, or drained and rinsed canned corn, or kernels cut from 3 ears of fresh corn

½ of a sweet red pepper, seeded and stemmed, finely chopped

½ of a small red onion, finely chopped

¼ cup chopped cilantro leaves, plus more sprigs for garnish

1 avocado, peeled, pitted, and sliced or cubed, for garnish

To prepare the dressing: In a small bowl, combine lime juice, olive oil, mustard, paprika, salt, and pepper; mix well with a fork or a whisk. Set aside.

In a large bowl, combine beans, corn, red pepper, onion, and cilantro. Add the dressing, gently folding to mix well. Taste and adjust seasoning, as desired. Spoon the salad onto a platter, and garnish with avocado and cilantro sprigs. Serve slightly chilled or at room temperature.

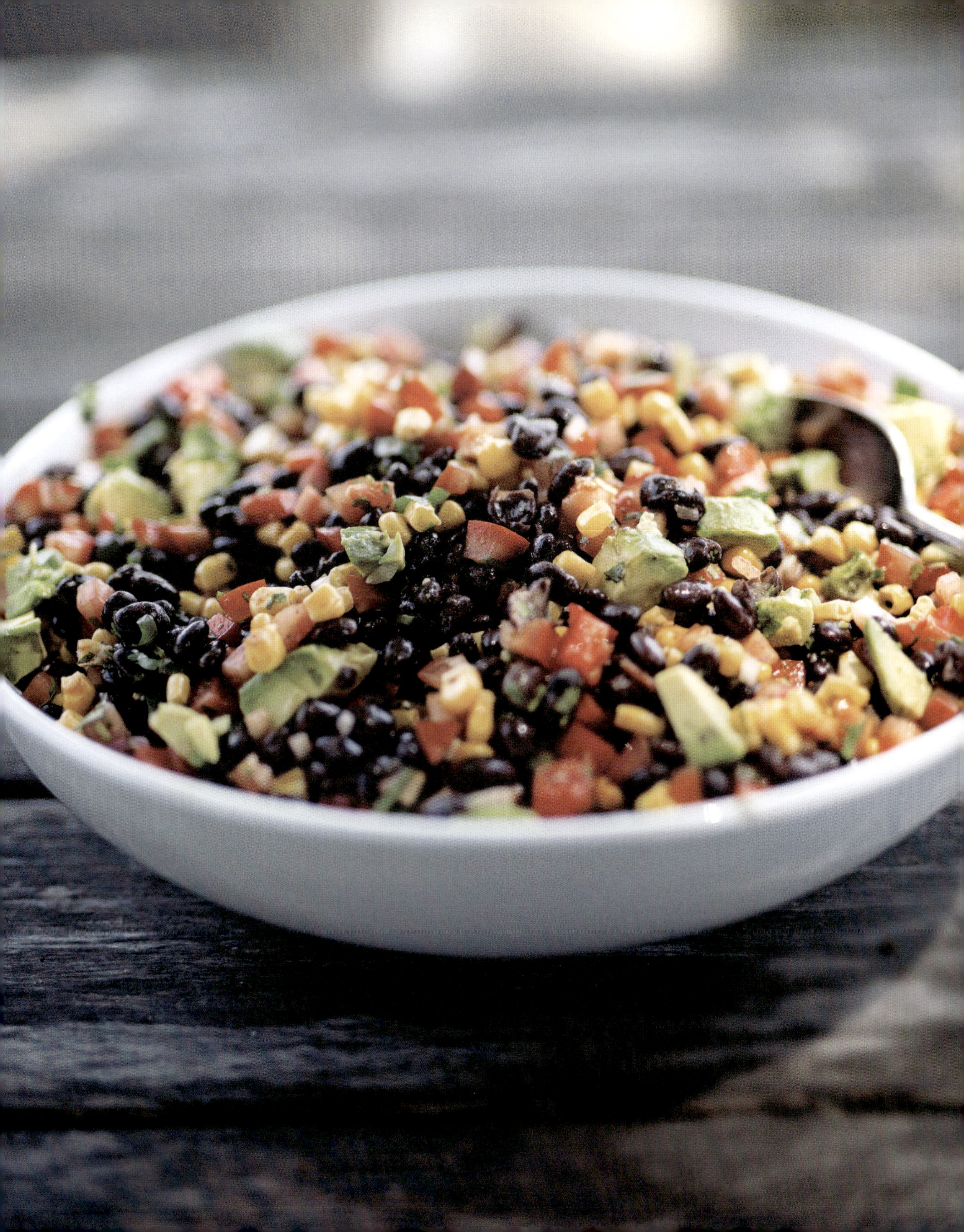

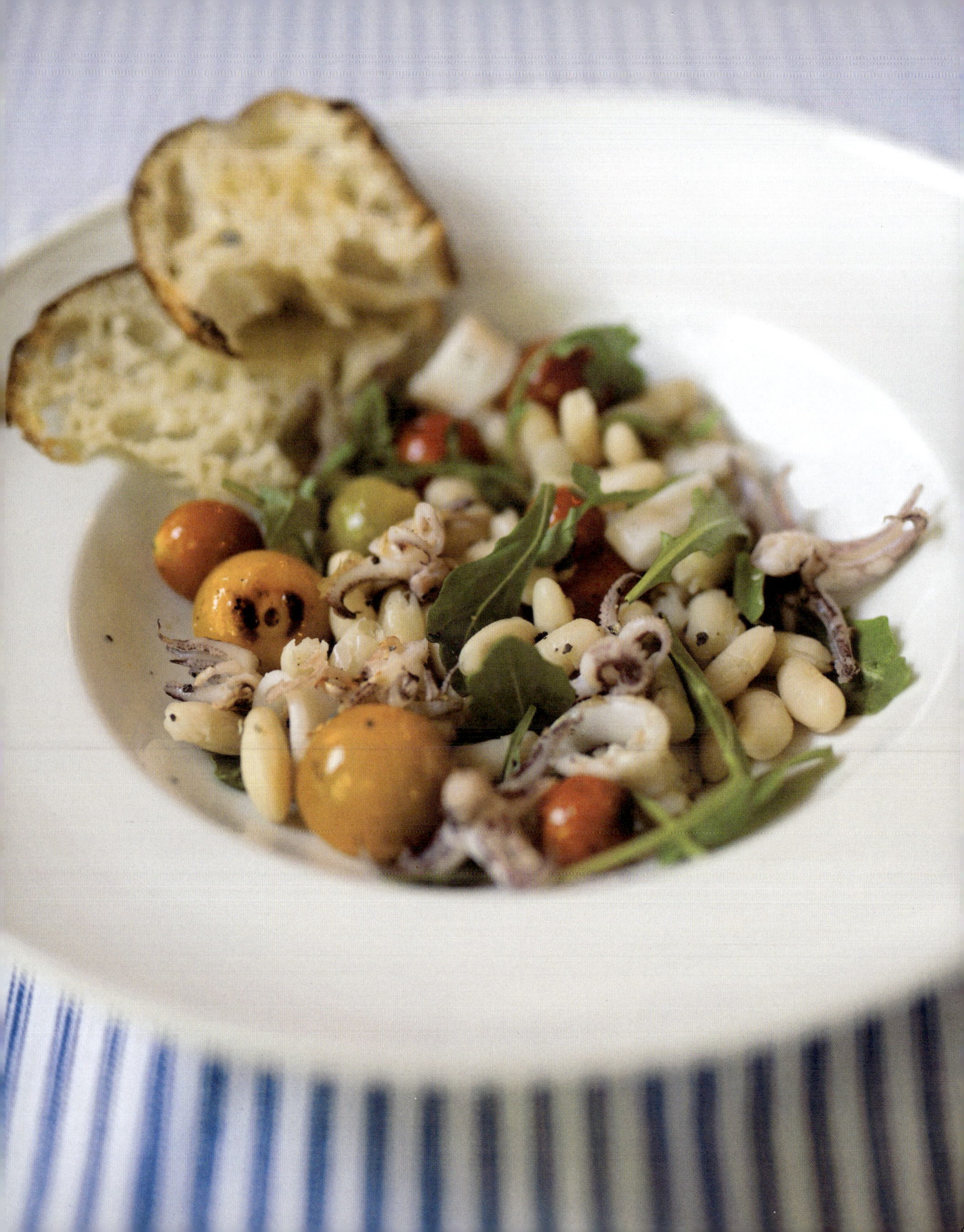

GRILLED CALAMARI *with* COCO BEANS *and* CHARRED TOMATOES

SERVES 4

Calamari is popular in France, especially along the Atlantic and Mediterranean coasts, and it is often prepared *a la planche* (grilled), either on its own or in combination with other seafood. It cooks almost instantly, so be sure to have the other ingredients already prepped. The juice from the grilled tomatoes will mingle with the vinaigrette to contribute a smoky flavor.

1 pound cleaned calamari, cut into bite-size rings and tentacles

2½ tablespoons extra-virgin olive oil (divided use)

1 teaspoon sea salt (divided use)

1 teaspoon freshly ground black pepper (divided use)

2 cups cherry tomatoes

¼ cup white wine vinegar

3 tablespoons lemon juice

1 tablespoon minced garlic

2 tablespoons minced flat-leaf parsley

2 tablespoons capers, rinsed and drained

⅓ cup green olives, pitted and chopped

3 cups cooked Coco beans (see page 26), or other white beans, such as Lingot or Cannellini, drained

2 cups baby arugula or wild arugula (optional)

In a bowl, combine calamari, 2 tablespoons olive oil, ½ teaspoon salt, and ½ teaspoon pepper; turn to coat. Let stand at room temperature for 10 to 15 minutes.

In another bowl, combine tomatoes with remaining ½ tablespoon oil; turn to coat. Let stand at room temperature for 10 to 15 minutes.

In a large salad bowl, combine vinegar, lemon juice, garlic, and a little salt and pepper. Mix well with a fork. Set aside.

Prepare a grill: Build a wood or charcoal fire, preheat a gas grill, or place a stove-top grill pan over medium-high heat. If using an outdoor grill, preheat a grill basket. Place calamari in the grill basket (or on the grill pan). Cook, turning several times, just until calamari is opaque and curls, about 1 minute. Transfer to a bowl. Place tomatoes in the grill basket (or on the grill pan) and cook, turning once or twice, until lightly charred, about 2 minutes.

In the salad bowl, add calamari, half the tomatoes, the parsley, capers, and olives to the dressing; toss to coat. Add beans and arugula, if using, and fold gently. Taste and adjust seasoning, as desired.

Spoon the salad onto a platter or 4 individual plates; garnish with remaining tomatoes.

CHICKPEAS with PROSCIUTTO, BLACK OLIVES, and CHERRY TOMATOES

SERVES 4

Nutty and slightly sweet, chickpeas are ideal in a salad. They hold their shape when cooked, and combine well with any number of other ingredients. Mixed cherry tomatoes make for a colorful salad, but red ones work fine if that's all you can find.

- 3 tablespoons extra-virgin olive oil
- 1 tablespoon red wine vinegar
- 3 cups cooked chickpeas (see page 26), drained
- 2 ounces thin-sliced prosciutto, cut into narrow strips
- ½ cup pitted oil-cured black olives, halved if desired
- 12 mixed heirloom cherry tomatoes, halved
- ½ cup minced red onion
- 2 tablespoons minced flat-leaf parsley
- Sea salt and freshly ground black pepper

In a salad bowl, combine olive oil and vinegar; mix well. Add chickpeas, prosciutto, olives, tomatoes, onion, and parsley; gently fold until well mixed. Taste and season with salt and pepper. Let stand at room temperature for 1 hour to allow flavors to blend.

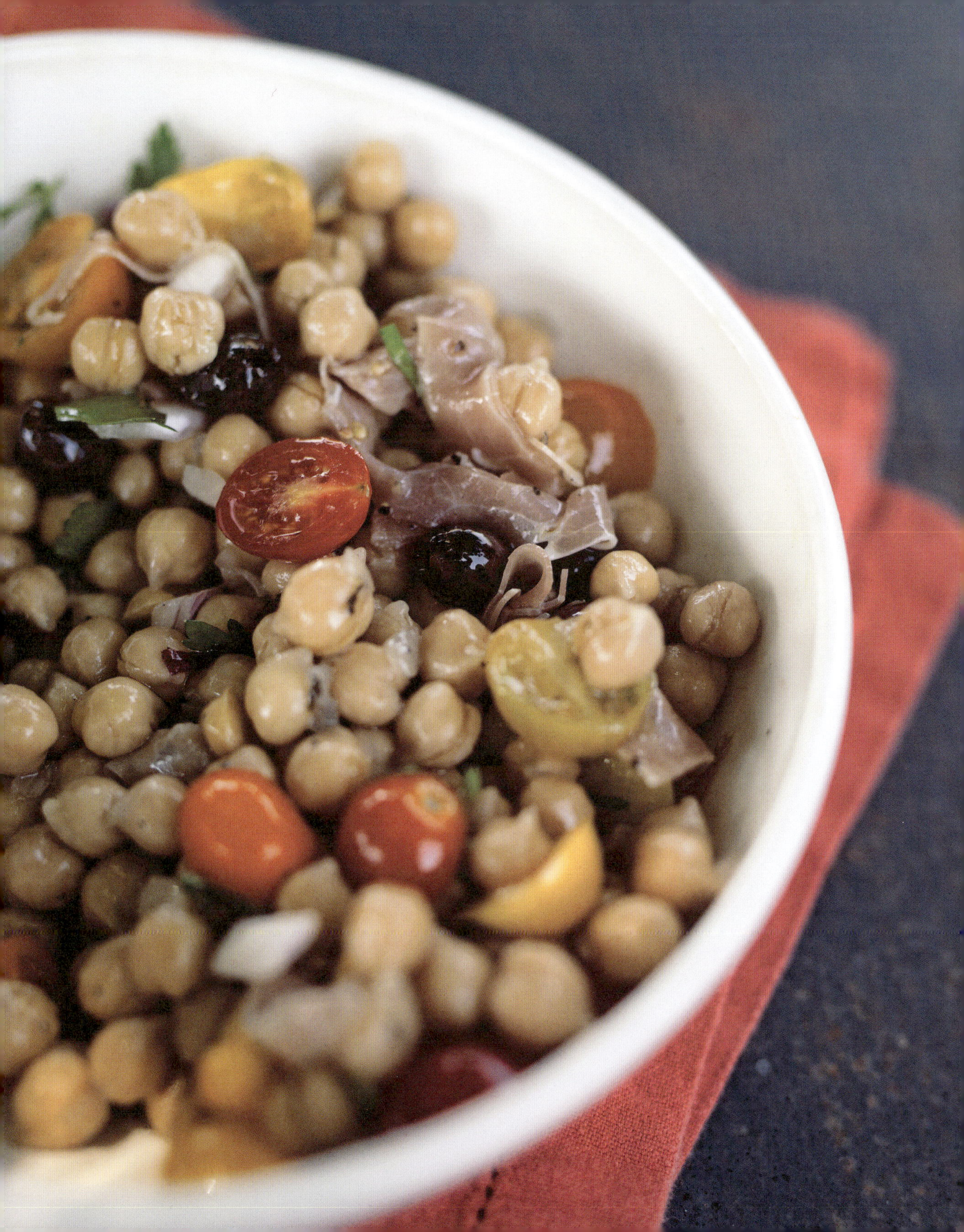

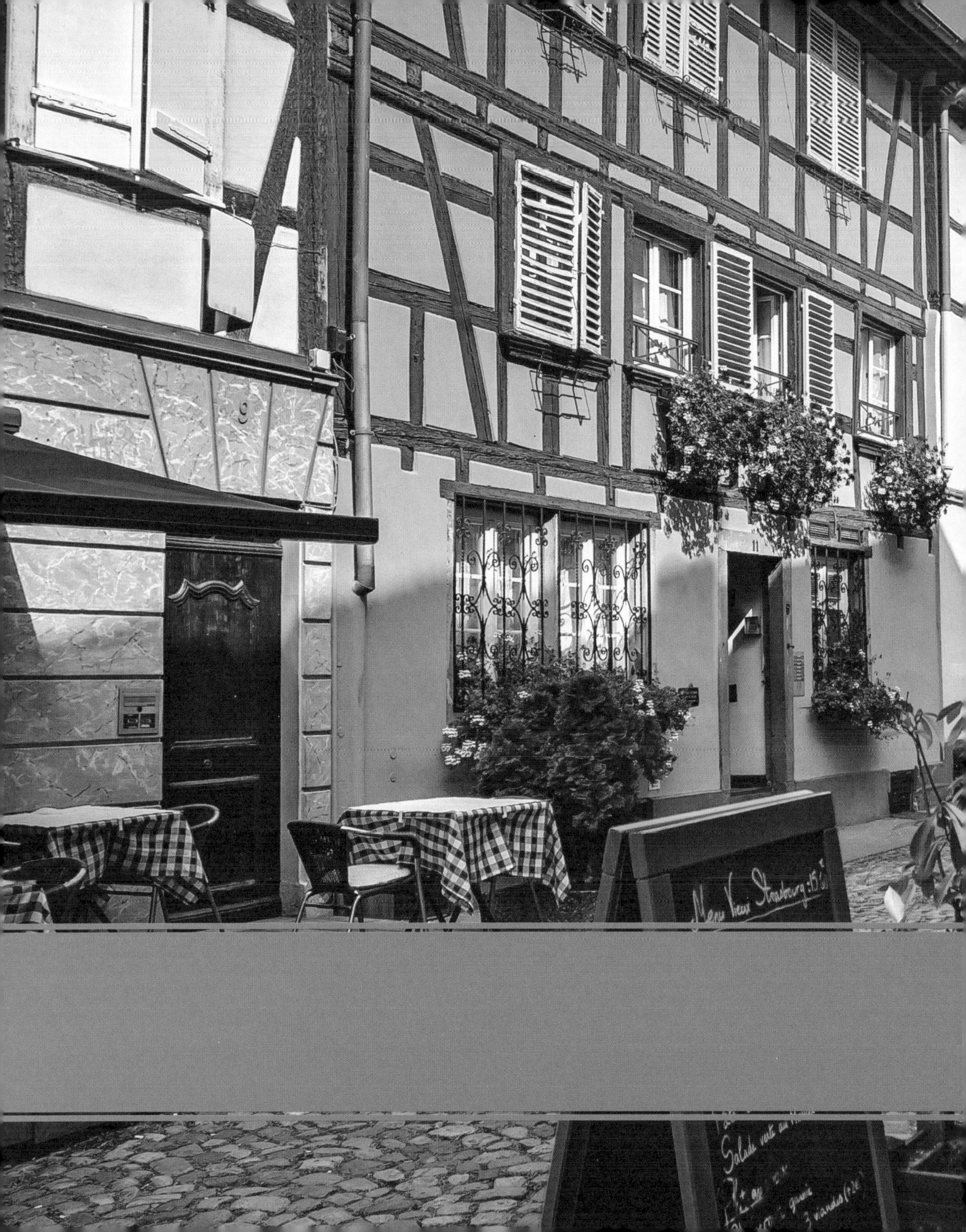
Menu Vieux Strasbourg

GRATINS, ROASTS & MAIN DISHES

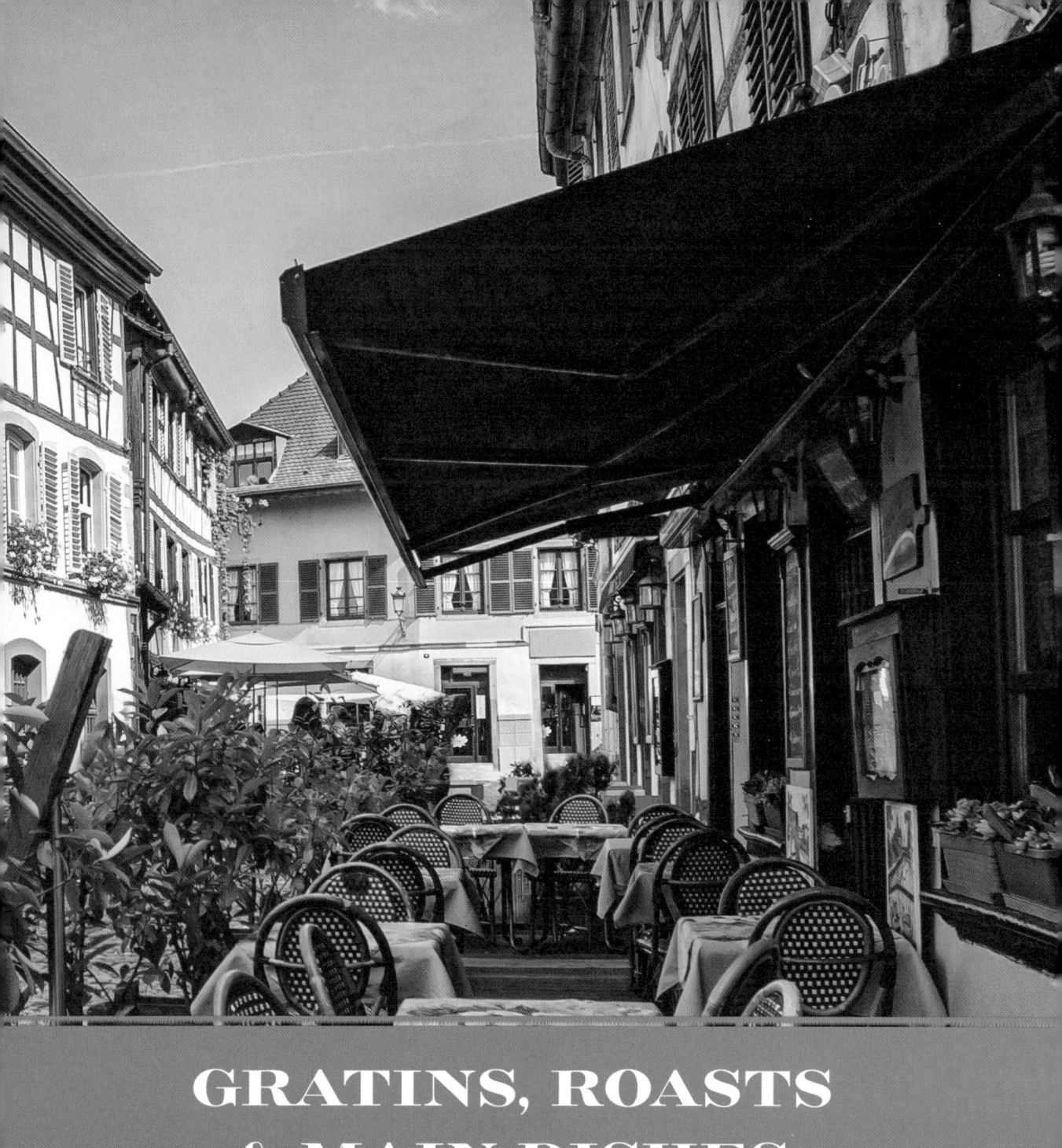

ROAST LEG OF LAMB WITH GARLIC, HERBS, AND FLAGEOLET BEANS
PAGE 72

The LAMB & FLAGEOLET LOVE AFFAIR

France is a notable lamb-raising country, with a history of sheep *troupeaux* (flocks) going back to Roman times. But the Flageolet bean didn't make its appearance until the middle of the 16th century, and it wasn't until the Chevrier Vert variety was developed in the late 1800s that the bean took the capital — and the population — by storm. It was the beginning of the lamb-and-Flageolet love affair, although in days gone by, people were more likely to cook with mature mutton than young lamb.

Flageolet beans and lamb go together. The small creamy bean and the rich ovine meat seem destined to be paired. Leg of Lamb with Flageolet Beans is a traditional centerpiece dish of Easter and Christmas meals in France, but it's also eaten throughout the year. Lamb chops, stews, and shoulder roasts, as well as riblets and shanks, are appreciated at any time and, like leg of lamb, are well-matched with Flageolets.

Lamb in France isn't just lamb. There are more than 2 dozen official lamb designations related to place, quality, and production methods (AOC, IGP, Label Rouge — see page 25) recognized by France and the European Union, including the famous *pré-salé* lambs of Normandy and the Bay of the Somme in Picardy. These lambs graze on the grasses of Atlantic coast salt-water marshes, which yield a distinct flavor. The Sisteron lambs, raised near my home in Provence, feed on wild thyme, winter savory, rosemary, and juniper of the mountains and hills of the Alpes-de-Haute-Provence, and have their own distinct savor as a result. From the Pyrenees to the Belgian border, from the Atlantic to the Alps, French shoppers can readily find local, quality-designated lamb.

Although most Flageolet beans are grown in the northern part of the country, home cooks can buy them everywhere, from tiny village groceries to huge urban supermarkets.

ROAST LEG OF LAMB with GARLIC, HERBS, AND FLAGEOLET BEANS

SERVES 8

This is one of the great classic dishes of France, a perennial Sunday lunch across the country as well as a holiday meal. French lambs — especially those with AOC, IGP, or Label Rouge designation — tend to be smaller than most American lambs. The legs generally weigh 4 to 5½ pounds, unlike many of our stateside lamb legs that tend to weigh closer to 7 pounds. I encourage you to seek out smaller-size roasts, even preordering from your butcher, as these will be more tender. However, if you can only find the larger ones, don't be dismayed. Lamb and beans are made for each other, regardless of size, and when the juices mingle and you take your first bite, you'll see why.

Begin by preparing the beans, as they will take longer to cook than the lamb. The beans can also be prepared a day ahead, and, once cooled, refrigerated in their broth. If you go this route, reheat gently, without overcooking, then proceed as below to finish and serve.

FOR THE BEANS

1 pound Flageolet beans, pale green if possible (see page 13), picked over and soaked (see page 26)

1 onion, peeled

2 cloves

1 fresh bay leaf (or ½ dried bay leaf)

3 to 4 fresh winter savory sprigs (or ½ teaspoon dried winter savory)

Freshly ground black pepper

1½ teaspoons sea salt

2 tablespoons unsalted butter, to finish

FOR THE LAMB

A 4½- to 5-pound leg of lamb

3 tablespoons extra-virgin olive oil (divided use)

1 tablespoon minced fresh thyme leaves

1 tablespoon minced fresh winter savory leaves (or 1 teaspoon dried winter savory)

2 teaspoons minced fresh rosemary, plus three 6-inch sprigs

Sea salt and freshly ground black pepper

3 to 4 garlic cloves (or more, as desired), thinly sliced

To prepare the beans: In a saucepan over medium-high heat, add beans and enough water to cover beans by about 3 inches. Stick the onion with the cloves, and add it to the beans and water, along with herbs and pepper. Bring to a boil, then reduce heat to low. Cook for 30 minutes, uncovered, skimming off any foam. Add salt; cover and continue to cook until beans are tender, about another hour. When beans are fully cooked, remove and discard onion, cloves, bay leaf, and savory sprigs. Set beans and broth aside.

Preheat oven to 400°F.

Trim any excess fat from the lamb, then rub all over with 2 tablespoons of olive oil. Season with thyme, winter savory, minced rosemary, and a generous amount of salt and pepper. Using a paring knife, make about 15 ½-inch-deep slits in the lamb. Insert a garlic sliver into each slit. Set the lamb in a shallow roasting pan.

Place the roasting pan in the preheated oven; roast for 30 minutes. Reduce heat to 350°F and continue roasting. Once or twice, dip rosemary sprigs in remaining olive oil and use them to baste the lamb. Roasting time is about 12 minutes per pound. The meat will be medium rare when an instant-read thermometer registers 130 to 135°F when inserted into the thickest part of the leg, but not touching the bone.

When lamb is done, remove it to a clean carving board, cover with foil, and let stand 15 minutes.

ROAST LEG OF LAMB *with* GARLIC, HERBS, AND FLAGEOLET BEANS

To finish, warm a serving platter. Drain beans, reserving broth for later use, if desired. In a clean saucepan over medium heat, add the drained beans and the butter. Simmer until heated through. Taste and adjust seasoning, as desired.

With a slotted spoon, spread buttered beans on the warmed platter. Carve the lamb, and arrange sliced lamb across the beans.

In a saucepan over medium-high heat, warm the cutting-board juices and any collected drippings from the roasting pan; drizzle over the lamb. Serve immediately.

TOMATO-BRAISED LAMB SHANKS
with FLAGEOLET BEANS

SERVES 4

Among the lesser cuts of lamb, shanks are one of the most rewarding. Long, slow cooking melts the meat off the bone, and allows the tendons and sinews to dissolve, contributing to an unctuous, thick sauce — in this case a tomato-based one — that blends with and enriches the Flageolet beans. Cooking the beans with fresh rosemary adds extra flavor to the final dish. Be sure to choose a Dutch oven that's large enough to hold the shanks in a single layer.

4 lamb shanks, each weighing between ¾ and 1 pound

Sea salt and freshly ground black pepper

1 tablespoon extra-virgin olive oil

1 medium onion, diced

1 large carrot, peeled and diced

1 celery stalk, diced

2 garlic cloves, minced

2 cups dry white wine

2 cups canned, whole tomatoes, chopped, with their juices

5 fresh thyme sprigs

2 fresh rosemary sprigs

¼ cup chopped flat-leaf parsley, to finish

FOR THE BEANS

½ pound Flageolet beans, pale green if possible (see page 13), picked over and soaked (see page 26)

2 fresh rosemary sprigs, about 5 inches long

1 teaspoon sea salt

Freshly ground black pepper

Preheat oven to 400°F.

Rub lamb shanks all over with salt and pepper. Place shanks on a baking sheet; roast in the preheated oven until browned and much of the fat is released, 20 to 30 minutes.

In a large Dutch oven over medium-high heat, warm the olive oil. Add onion; sauté until translucent, about 2 minutes. Add carrots, celery, and garlic; sauté until vegetables begin to color slightly, about 2 minutes more. Increase heat to high and add wine, scraping up any clinging vegetable bits. Simmer until the mixture is reduced by half, then add tomatoes and their juice, thyme, and rosemary, stirring to combine. Tuck the lamb shanks into the tomato mixture. Cover and bake until the meat easily pulls from the bone, 1½ to 2 hours.

Meanwhile, in a saucepan over medium-high heat, combine drained beans, rosemary, and enough water to cover beans by about 3 inches. Bring to a boil, then reduce heat to low. Simmer, uncovered, for 30 minutes, skimming off any foam. Add salt and pepper; cover and continue to cook until beans are tender, about another hour. Discard rosemary and set beans in their broth aside.

TOMATO-BRAISED LAMB SHANKS
with FLAGEOLET BEANS

When shanks are ready to serve, warm a platter or 4 individual shallow bowls or dinner plates. Gently simmer beans over low heat until warmed through, about 10 minutes. Taste and adjust seasoning, as desired.

Remove shanks to a large bowl; cover loosely with aluminum foil.

Using a slotted spoon, add the beans to the tomato sauce. Using a wooden spoon to keep from breaking the beans, fold them gently into the sauce. Arrange sauced beans on the warmed serving platter (or on individual bowls or dinner plates) and top with the shanks, bone-end up. Sprinkle with minced parsley and serve immediately.

LAMB STEW with FLAGEOLET BEANS

SERVES 4 TO 6

Flageolet beans and lamb go together perfectly in this very simple, country-style stew, thick and rich. Serve with plenty of crusty country-style bread to soak up the juices.

FOR THE BEANS

½ pound Flageolet beans, picked over, soaked, and drained (see page 26)

2 fresh winter savory sprigs (or ¼ teaspoon dried winter savory)

1 fresh bay leaf (or ½ dried bay leaf)

1 teaspoon sea salt

¼ teaspoon freshly ground black pepper

FOR THE LAMB

2 pounds lamb shoulder, cut into 2-inch pieces

Sea salt and freshly ground black pepper

3 tablespoons extra-virgin olive oil

1 medium onion, chopped

3 garlic cloves, chopped

1 carrot, peeled and chopped

1 leek, white part only, chopped

1 sweet red pepper, seeded and stemmed, cut into 1-inch pieces

1 cup dry white wine

Bouquet garni: 2 thyme sprigs, 4 flat-leaf parsley sprigs, and 2 fresh (or 1 dried) bay leaves, tied with kitchen string

3 peeled tomatoes, seeded and chopped, with juice

2 cups homemade chicken broth (or low-salt commercial broth)

1 tablespoon unsalted butter

In a saucepan over medium-high heat, add the beans, savory, and bay leaf, plus enough water to cover beans by about 3 inches. Bring to a boil, then reduce heat to low. Simmer, uncovered, for 30 minutes, skimming off any foam. Add salt and pepper; cover and continue to cook until beans are tender, about 1 hour. When beans are tender, discard winter savory and bay leaf. Set beans and their broth aside.

Preheat oven to 350°F.

Season the lamb well with salt and pepper. In a large Dutch oven over medium-high heat, warm the olive oil. Add the meat a few pieces at a time, searing in several batches until nicely browned on all sides; do not crowd the pan. With a slotted spoon, remove the meat to a clean bowl, and repeat for the remaining batches, adding more olive oil if needed. When all meat is seared, add onions, garlic, carrots, leeks, and red pepper to the pan, sautéing until onion and leeks are translucent, about 2 minutes. Remove vegetables to the bowl with the lamb. Increase heat to high and add wine, scraping up any clinging bits of meat.

Return meat and vegetables to the pan. Add the bouquet garni, chopped tomatoes and their juice, and chicken broth. Cover and place in the preheated oven. Braise, stirring from time to time, until the meat is easily pierced with a fork, about 1 hour. Discard the bouquet garni.

When meat is tender, drain beans, reserving the broth for another use, if desired. Using a wooden spoon to keep from breaking the beans, fold them gently into the sauce along with the butter. Serve hot into bowls.

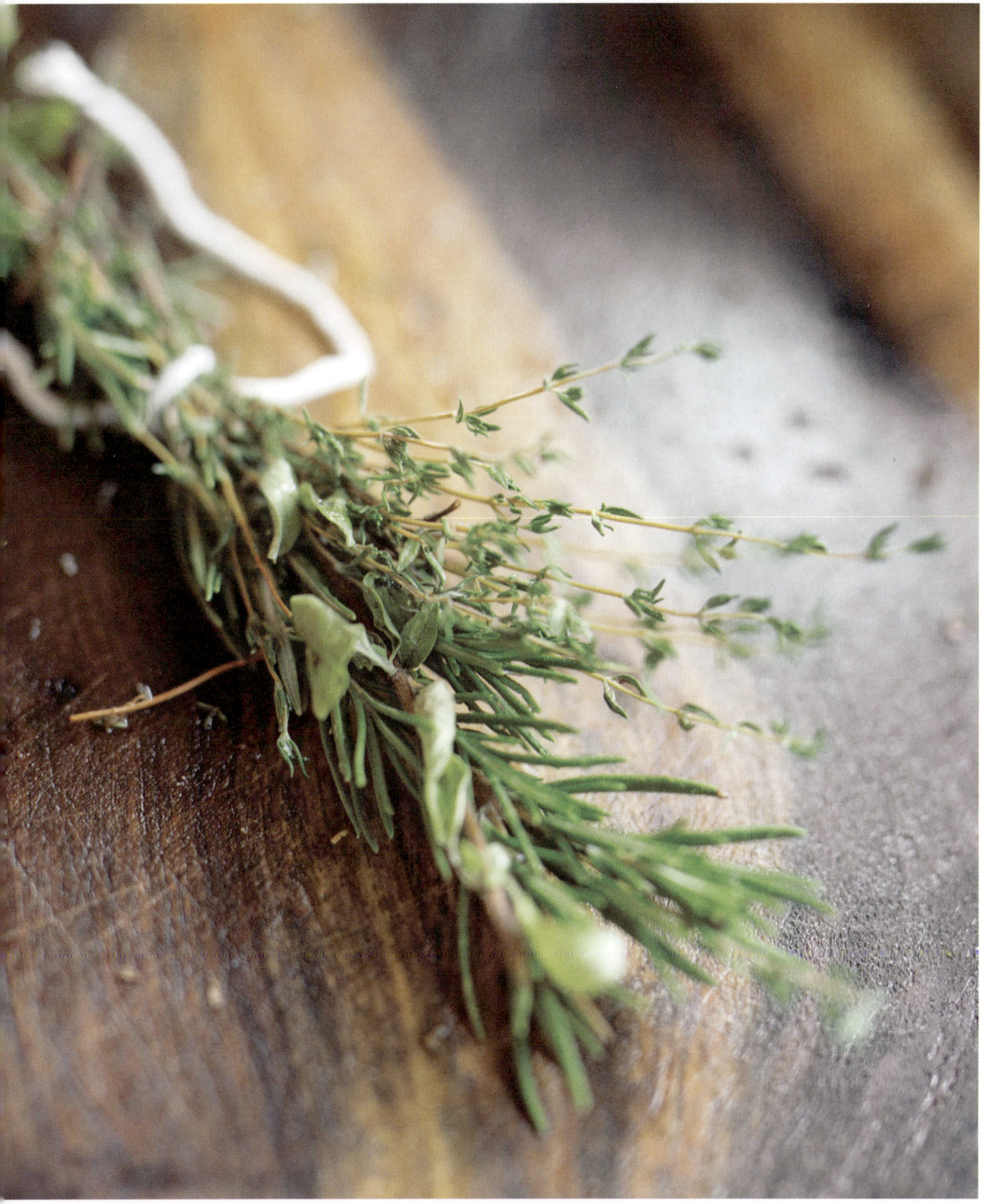

GRATIN OF LEEKS and WHITE BEANS with GRUYÈRE

SERVES 2 TO 4

This preparation is reminiscent of one of my favorite French dishes, Leek and Salt Cod Gratin. But here, I've used beans instead of salt cod to make a vegetarian version. This can be served either as a main dish or a side dish. Feel free to use other white beans, as well. It will serve 3 to 4 people as a side dish, or 2 to 3 as a main dish.

5 tablespoons unsalted butter (divided use), plus more for the baking dish

5 large leeks, white and light-green parts only, minced

½ teaspoon sea salt

2 cups cooked Lingot, Cannellini, or Royal Corona beans (see page 26), drained and kept warm

2 tablespoons heavy cream

1 teaspoon chopped fresh thyme leaves (or ¼ teaspoon dried thyme)

¼ teaspoon freshly ground black pepper

½ to ¾ cup fresh bread crumbs

¾ cup grated Gruyère cheese

Preheat oven to 400°F.

In a skillet over medium-high heat, melt 3 tablespoons butter. When it foams, add leeks and salt; sauté until leeks are soft and translucent, about 10 minutes. In a bowl, combine leeks and beans with cream, thyme, and pepper; mash with a fork or potato masher to a chunky consistency. Taste and adjust seasoning, as desired.

Butter a 1-quart baking dish, then spread the bean mixture evenly into the dish.

In a small skillet over medium-high heat, melt remaining 2 tablespoons butter. When it foams, add bread crumbs and stir, frying until light golden. Sprinkle fried bread crumbs over the bean mixture, then top with grated Gruyère cheese.

Place in the preheated oven and bake until the edges bubble and the mixture is hot, 15 to 20 minutes. Serve hot.

HACHIS PARMENTIER

SERVES 4

One of the great French comfort foods, Hachis Parmentier is essentially a French version of Shepherd's Pie using ground beef. A well-seasoned mixture of beef, carrots, and onions is usually topped with a thick layer of fluffy mashed potatoes, then scattered with grated cheese and browned in the oven. Puréed white beans easily replace potatoes and make for a lighter version of the classic.

FOR THE FILLING

1½ tablespoons unsalted butter

2 onions, finely chopped

2 garlic cloves, minced

1 carrot, peeled and finely chopped

1 pound ground beef

½ cup chopped flat-leaf parsley

½ teaspoon herbes de Provence

½ teaspoon sea salt

½ teaspoon freshly ground black pepper

⅓ cup chopped canned tomatoes with their juice

FOR THE BEANS

3 cups cooked white beans, such as Tarbais, Cassoulet, or Royal Corona (see page 26), drained

2 tablespoons unsalted butter

2 tablespoons heavy cream

½ teaspoon sea salt

½ teaspoon freshly ground black pepper

TO FINISH

¼ cup grated Parmesan cheese

¼ cup grated Gruyère cheese

1 tablespoon unsalted butter

Preheat oven to 400°F.

In a skillet over medium-high heat, melt 1½ tablespoons butter. Sauté onions, garlic, and carrots until soft, about 10 minutes. Crumble ground beef and add it to the pan; sauté until lightly browned, about 5 minutes. Add parsley, herbes de Provence, salt, and pepper; stir well. Add tomatoes and stir, cooking another 2 to 3 minutes.

Spread meat mixture in a large loaf pan or other baking dish. Set aside.

In the bowl of a food processor, combine beans, 2 tablespoons butter, cream, salt, and pepper; process until smooth. (Alternatively, purée using a stand mixer or hand mixer.) Taste and adjust seasoning, as desired. If the mixture seems too thick, add a little more cream.

Spread bean mixture evenly on top of the meat mixture. Sprinkle with cheeses and dot with butter.

Place the baking dish in the preheated oven; bake until the edges bubble and the top forms a golden crust, about 20 minutes.

Remove the dish from the oven and let rest 5 to 10 minutes before serving. Use a spatula to cut and serve 2-inch slices, or use a serving spoon to scoop out each serving.

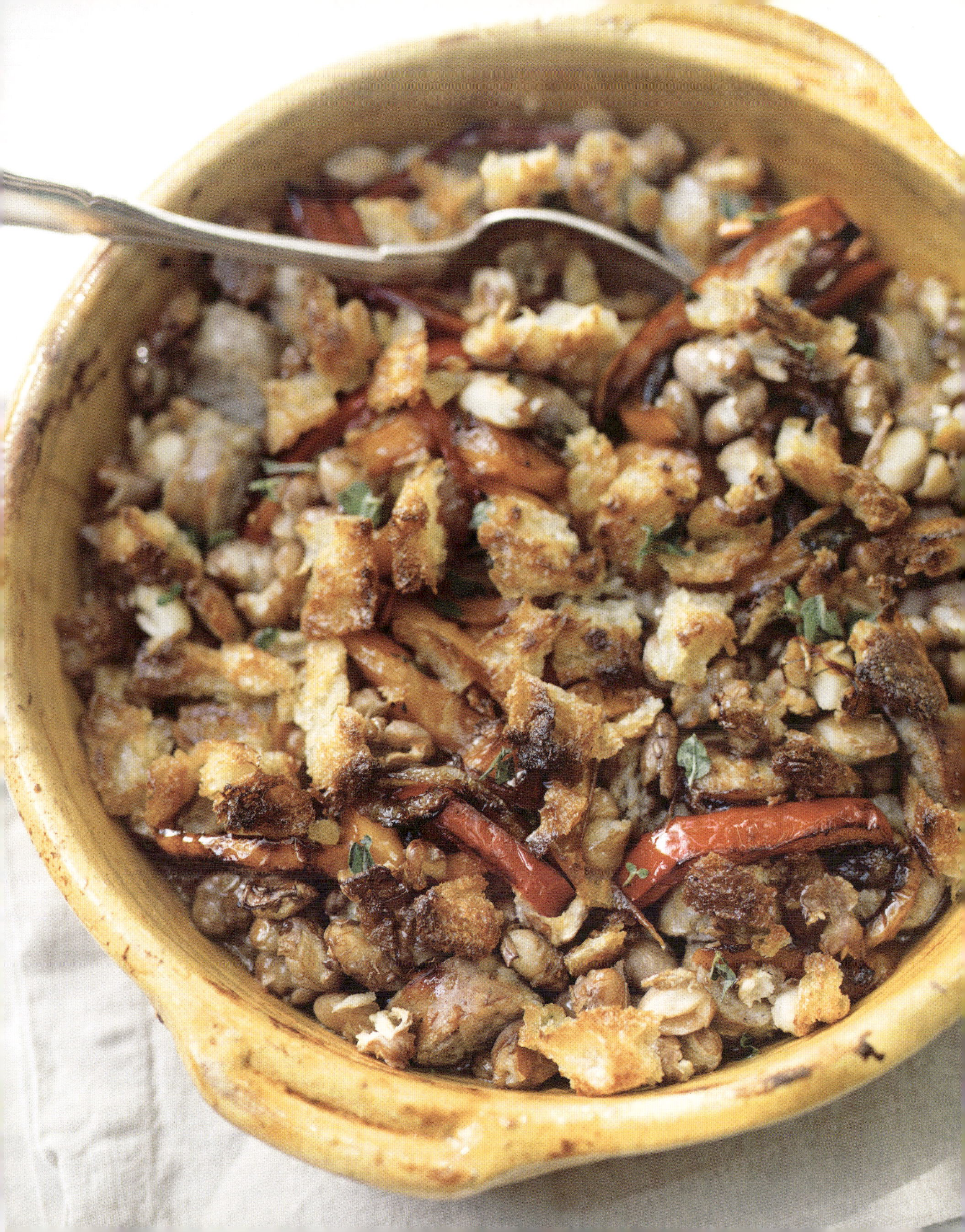

GRATIN OF CRANBERRY BEANS, SWEET PEPPERS, and TOULOUSE SAUSAGE

SERVES 4

Fresh Cranberry beans appear in French markets in the fall for a brief window, but local cooks use dried beans to make this dish year round. Saffron and cumin give the juices a golden hue and a hint of mystery, and sausages contribute their own flavors to the whole.

2 tablespoons unsalted butter

½ cup fresh bread crumbs

1 tablespoon plus ¼ cup extra-virgin olive oil (divided use)

4 Toulouse sausages (or substitute mild Italian sausage links)

½ of an onion, thinly sliced

1 sweet red pepper, seeded and stemmed, sliced lengthwise into thin strips

1 yellow or orange bell pepper, seeded and stemmed, sliced lengthwise into thin strips

3 cups cooked Cranberry beans (see page 26), with broth

Sea salt and freshly ground black pepper

Pinch of saffron

¼ teaspoon ground cumin

1 tablespoon fresh oregano (divided use)

Preheat oven to 400°F.

In a small skillet over medium-high heat, melt butter. Add bread crumbs and stir, frying until light golden. Set aside.

In a skillet over medium-high heat, warm 1 tablespoon olive oil. Add sausages; cook, turning often, until browned and cooked through, about 10 minutes. Remove sausages and their juices to a bowl. Return the pan to medium-high heat; add remaining ¼ cup olive oil. When oil is hot, add onions. Reduce heat to medium and cook until onions begin to soften, about 3 minutes. Add peppers and continue to cook, stirring as needed, until onions and peppers are very soft, about 15 minutes. Reduce heat as needed to prevent browning.

In a gratin dish, add onions, peppers, and their cooking juices. With a slotted spoon, add beans, reserving bean broth. Turn beans several times, and add a tablespoon or two of reserved broth. Add salt and pepper, saffron, cumin, and just over half of the oregano.

Cut sausages into 1-inch pieces, reserving juice; add sausage to the gratin dish, along with a tablespoon of cooking juices. Taste and adjust seasoning, as desired.

Scatter with buttered bread crumbs. (They will not make a solid layer.)

Place the gratin in the preheated oven; cook until the surface bubbles and bread crumbs are golden brown, about 15 minutes. Remove and sprinkle with remaining oregano.

Serve hot directly from the gratin dish.

CHICKPEA and LAMB GRATIN with HARISSA

SERVES 4

Chickpeas are grown in southern France, an area that — much like North Africa — produces a lot of lamb as well as olive oil, onions, garlic, and tomatoes. The seasonings — cumin, cayenne pepper, and harissa — reflect this influence, too. Fried bread crumbs make the crunchy topping.

1 sweet red pepper

½ teaspoon ground cumin

¼ teaspoon cayenne pepper

1 teaspoon sea salt

1 pound lamb shoulder, cubed

5 tablespoons extra-virgin olive oil (divided use)

½ of an onion, thinly sliced

1 garlic clove, minced

4 tablespoons tomato paste

1 to 2 teaspoons harissa

1 teaspoon fresh thyme (or ½ teaspoon dried thyme)

3 cups cooked chickpeas (see page 26), drained

1 cup fresh bread crumbs

Preheat oven to 400°F.

Under a broiler (or on a stove-top grill), roast red pepper until charred, turning often. Place pepper in a heavy paper bag and let stand at least 10 minutes and up to 30. Remove pepper and slip off charred skin. Cut pepper in half and remove ribs and seeds. Cut pepper lengthwise into thin strips. Set aside.

In a small bowl, combine cumin, cayenne, and salt.

In a large bowl, drizzle lamb with 1 tablespoon olive oil, then season with spice mixture, thoroughly coating cubes. Set aside for 30 minutes.

In a large skillet over medium-high heat, warm 2 teaspoons olive oil. Add meat; brown well, turning often, until a crust forms, about 6 minutes. Remove meat to a clean bowl and set aside.

Adding more olive oil to the skillet, if needed, sauté onions until nearly translucent, then add garlic; sauté 1 to 2 minutes. Add tomato paste and harissa, and stir. Add thyme and ½ cup water; stir, scraping up any clinging bits of meat. Reduce heat to medium-low; simmer until a light sauce forms, about 4 minutes. Add chickpeas to sauce, stirring gently. Simmer for 3 to 4 minutes. Taste and adjust seasoning, as desired.

Spoon chickpea mixture into a gratin or other shallow baking dish; add pepper strips, lamb, and meat juices.

In a small skillet over medium-high heat, warm remaining 2 tablespoons olive oil. Add bread crumbs and stir, frying until light golden.

Sprinkle fried bread crumbs across the surface of the chickpea-and-lamb mixture and place in the preheated oven. Bake until the top is golden brown and the sauce bubbles, 15 to 20 minutes.

Serve immediately, directly from the baking dish.

BRAISED CHICKEN THIGHS with CRANBERRY BEANS and BASIL

SERVES 4

Meaty Cranberry beans soak up the chicken and tomato juices, while basil sprigs — added in quantity at the end of cooking — act as an integral part of the dish rather than mere seasoning.

6 bone-in, skin-on chicken thighs

½ teaspoon sea salt

½ teaspoon freshly ground black pepper

2 tablespoons extra-virgin olive oil

1 small onion, chopped

2 garlic cloves, minced

1 teaspoon chopped fresh thyme (or ½ teaspoon dried thyme)

½ cup dry white wine

3 tomatoes, chopped, juice reserved

2 cups cooked Cranberry beans (see page 26), with broth

1 bunch basil, coarse stem ends removed, small leaves reserved for garnish

2 tablespoons basil-infused olive oil

Season chicken with salt and pepper. In a heavy bottomed saucepan or Dutch oven over medium-high heat, warm the olive oil. Add chicken and brown, turning several times, until skin is crisp and golden, about 10 minutes.

Remove chicken from the pan and reserve on a plate. Add onion and garlic to the pan. Reduce heat to medium; sauté until onions are nearly translucent, about 3 minutes. Add thyme, white wine, and tomatoes and their juice, scraping up any clinging bits of meat. Return chicken to the pan, crispy side up. Cover, reduce heat to low, and cook until chicken is tender, about 35 minutes. Remove chicken to a plate and keep warm.

Add beans and 3 tablespoons of bean broth to tomato mixture, and fold gently. Increase heat to medium and simmer to reduce the sauce slightly; It should be thickish, with a cream-like consistency. Taste and adjust seasoning, as desired. Gently fold in basil sprigs, and simmer just until the basil leaves wilt but remain bright green, about 2 minutes.

To serve, spoon some of the tomato, bean, and basil mixture onto 4 plates; top each with a piece of chicken. Drizzle beans with a little basil-infused olive oil, and garnish with reserved basil leaves.

BASQUE-STYLE BEANS *with* STANDING PORK RIB ROAST

SERVES 6

Alubia Blanca — a small white bean much favored in the Basque regions of both France and Spain — forms the base of this popular dish. The beans are slowly cooked with a little pork belly, vegetables, and herbs before being given a spicy finish of Piment d'Espelette, the famous Basque pepper. These beans can be served on their own or as an accompaniment to almost any dish, but serving them with pork roast makes a special-occasion meal.

FOR THE BEANS

½ pound Alubia Blanca, Lingot, Tarbais, Cassoulet, or Cannellini beans, picked over and soaked (see page 26)

¼ pound skinless pork belly, cut into ½-inch pieces

1 onion, thinly sliced

1 leek, white and light-green parts only, thinly sliced

2 carrots, peeled and cut into ½-inch rounds

2 large tomatoes, quartered

2 tablespoons minced flat-leaf parsley

4 fresh thyme sprigs

2 fresh rosemary sprigs

2 fresh bay leaves (or 1 dried bay leaf)

2 garlic cloves, crushed

8 cups cold water

2 to 3 teaspoons sea salt

2 teaspoons Piment d'Espelette

FOR THE ROAST

A 4-rib pork roast (about 3 pounds)

3 or 4 fresh rosemary sprigs

1 tablespoon coarse sea salt

½ tablespoon freshly ground black pepper

1 teaspoon Piment d'Espelette

1 to 1½ tablespoons unsalted butter

2 onions, sliced

4 garlic cloves, crushed

¼ cup water

In a saucepan over medium-high heat, add beans and enough water to cover beans by about 2 inches. Bring to a boil, then reduce heat to low and simmer for 10 minutes. Set aside.

In a Dutch oven (or other large, heavy pot) over medium heat, sauté pork belly until some of its fat renders, about 2 to 3 minutes. Add onions, leek, carrots, tomatoes, parsley, thyme, rosemary, and bay leaves. Continue to cook, stirring, until onions and leek are translucent, about 5 minutes.

Drain beans and add them to the large pot. Add garlic and 8 cups of water. Bring the pot back to boiling, then reduce heat to low; simmer, partially covered, for 30 minutes. Add 2 teaspoons of salt and continue to simmer until beans are tender, about 1½ to 2 hours. Add Piment d'Espelette, gently stirring to combine. Taste and adjust seasoning, as desired.

While the beans are cooking, preheat oven to 475°F. Dry the roast well, and rub all over with rosemary sprigs; set sprigs aside. In a small bowl, mix together salt, pepper, and Piment d'Espelette. Rub the roast all over with the mixture.

In a large, heavy-bottomed Dutch oven over medium heat, melt the butter. Increase heat to high, and place the roast, fat side down, in the pan; sear until well browned. Turn, searing the sides, ends, and even the bone side. This will take about 10 minutes. Remove browned roast to a bowl and set aside.

BASQUE-STYLE BEANS *with* STANDING
PORK RIB ROAST

Reduce heat to medium; add onions to the pan, stirring and scraping up any clinging bits of meat. (If pan is dry, add remaining butter.) Continue sautéing until onions are translucent, about 4 minutes; add garlic. Add ¼ cup water and stir well. Place reserved rosemary stems on top of the onions, then top with the roast, bone-side down. Cover and place in the preheated oven.

Cook the covered roast for 15 minutes, then reduce heat to 325°F. Cook until an instant-read thermometer registers 140 to 145°F when inserted into the thickest part of the roast, but not touching the bones, about 45 minutes longer.

To serve, carve meat away from the bones, then into ½-inch slices, reserving juices. With a slotted spoon, place half the beans onto a deep serving platter. Arrange pork slices atop the beans, and drizzle with reserved meat juices. Serve the remaining beans on the side.

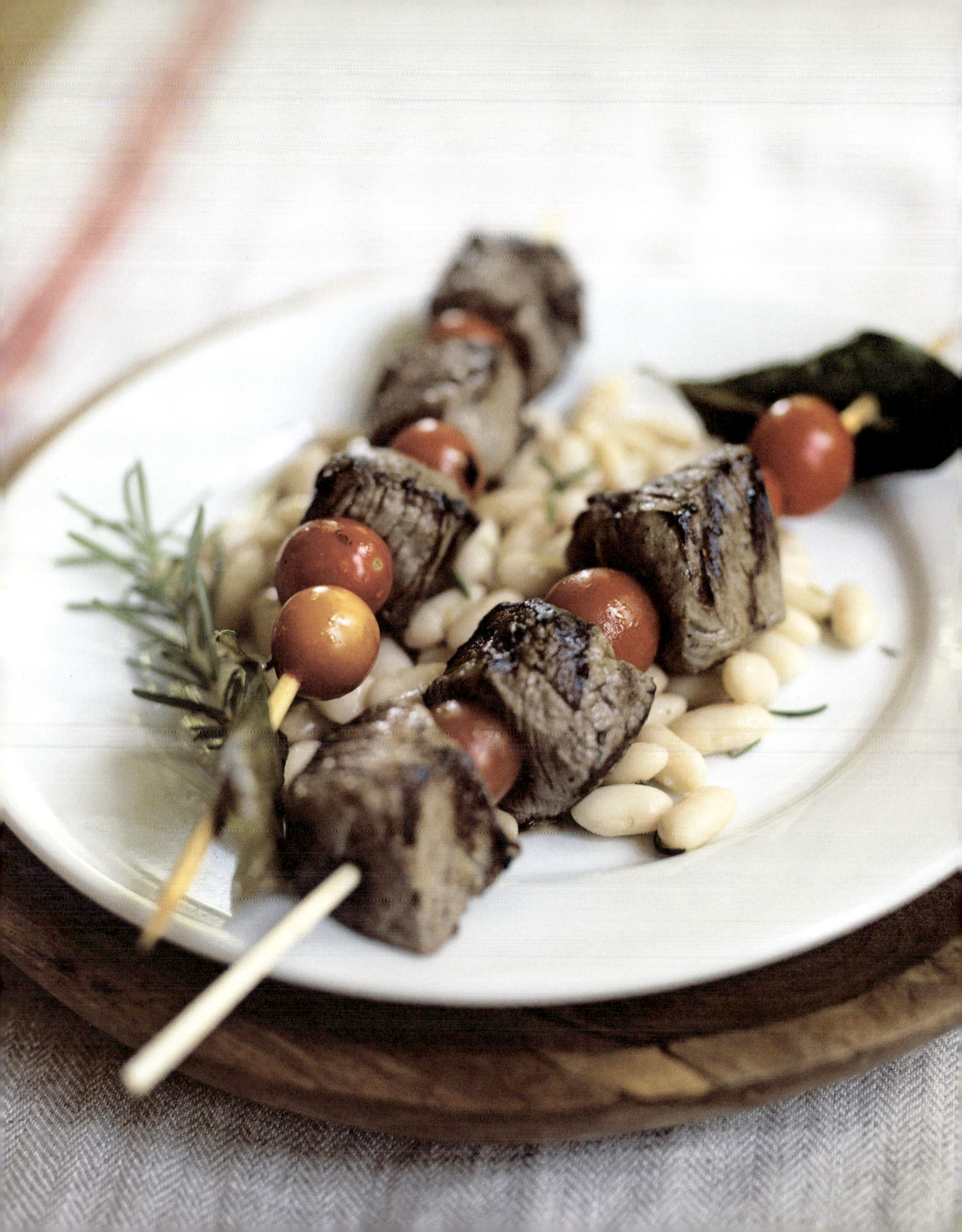

ROSEMARY WHITE BEANS *with* BEEF *and* CHERRY TOMATO BROCHETTES

SERVES 4

The rosemary does double duty here, infusing the beans and marinating the beef. Rosemary is an important herb in southern France and people frequently have a plant or two growing near the house.

FOR THE BEANS

1 tablespoon extra-virgin olive oil

1 small onion, finely chopped

2 garlic cloves, crushed and finely chopped

3 fresh rosemary sprigs, about 6 inches long

1 bay leaf

½ pound white beans, such as Tarbais, Royal Corona, or Cannellini, picked over and rinsed

2 teaspoons sea salt

1 teaspoon freshly ground black pepper

FOR THE BROCHETTES

2 pounds beef sirloin or other tender steak, cut into 1½-inch cubes

3 tablespoons extra-virgin olive oil

3 fresh rosemary sprigs, about 6 inches long

1 teaspoon freshly ground black pepper (divided use)

1 bay leaf

2 pints cherry tomatoes

1 to 1½ teaspoons sea salt

In a soup pot or large casserole over medium-high heat, warm the olive oil. Add onion and sauté until translucent, about 3 minutes, then add garlic and sauté another minute. Add rosemary, bay leaf, and beans. Add enough water to cover beans by about 2 inches and bring to a boil. Reduce heat to low, partially cover, and simmer for 1 hour. Add salt and pepper, and more water as needed. Continue to simmer until beans are tender, another 30 to 60 minutes, depending on the size of the beans. Taste and adjust seasoning, as desired. Set aside.

In a baking dish or bowl, combine steak cubes, olive oil, rosemary, ½ teaspoon pepper, and bay leaf; toss well to coat. Marinate at room temperature for an hour, stirring from time to time.

Prepare a grill: Build a wood or charcoal fire, preheat a gas grill, or place a stove-top grill pan over medium-high heat.

Thread steak and tomatoes onto eight 12-inch skewers, alternating them. (If using wood skewers, you will need to soak them first in water.) Sprinkle brochettes with salt and remaining ½ teaspoon of pepper.

Place brochettes on the hot grill; cook, turning once or twice until meat is seared and tomato skins start to pop, about 5 minutes.

To serve, spoon beans onto 4 dinner plates and top each serving with two brochettes.

SEA BASS ON A BED of PURÉED WHITE BEANS

SERVES 4

The white beans are whipped to a pillowy consistency, flavored with olive oil that's infused with garlic and fresh thyme, then topped with seared sea bass. It is elegant in its simplicity, the sort of dish you might find in a fine restaurant in the South of France, home to olive oil and Mediterranean fish. For a final dash of style and texture, the finished dish is garnished with a tangle of frisée (also known as curly endive).

FOR THE BEANS

Scant ¼ cup extra-virgin olive oil, plus more for drizzling

1 garlic clove, crushed

6 fresh thyme sprigs

½ pound Royal Corona, Tarbais, or Cassoulet beans, cooked (see page 26), with broth

½ teaspoon sea salt

¼ teaspoon freshly ground black pepper

FOR THE FISH

4 sea bass fillets, each about 5 to 6 ounces and ¾- to 1-inch thick

1 teaspoon sea salt

1 teaspoon freshly ground black pepper

1 tablespoon unsalted butter

1 tablespoon extra-virgin olive oil

TO FINISH

1 head frisée, pale yellow inner leaves only

To prepare beans: In a small saucepan over medium-high heat, warm olive oil with garlic and thyme. Reduce heat to medium; simmer for 5 minutes, and discard thyme.

In the bowl of a food processor, combine beans, garlic, and herb-infused olive oil; process until smooth. (Alternatively, purée ingredients using a hand mixer or even a potato masher for a more rustic effect.) Add salt and pepper, and process again. Taste and adjust seasoning, as desired. The purée should be creamy but not soupy. If it seems too thick, add a little reserved bean broth. Keep bean purée warm while preparing fish.

To prepare fish: In a large bowl, sprinkle fillets with salt and pepper, turning several times to coat. Set aside.

In a skillet over medium-high heat, melt butter and olive oil until the mixture foams. Add fish and cook until the bottom surfaces are golden and lower parts of the fillets turn opaque, about 5 minutes. Turn and cook the other side until golden, another 4 minutes; fish should now be entirely opaque and easily flake with a fork.

Spoon some hot, puréed beans onto 4 dinner plates or shallow rimmed bowls. Top each serving of beans with a piece of fish. Drizzle a little olive oil around the edge of the beans, and place a tangle of frisée on top of the fish.

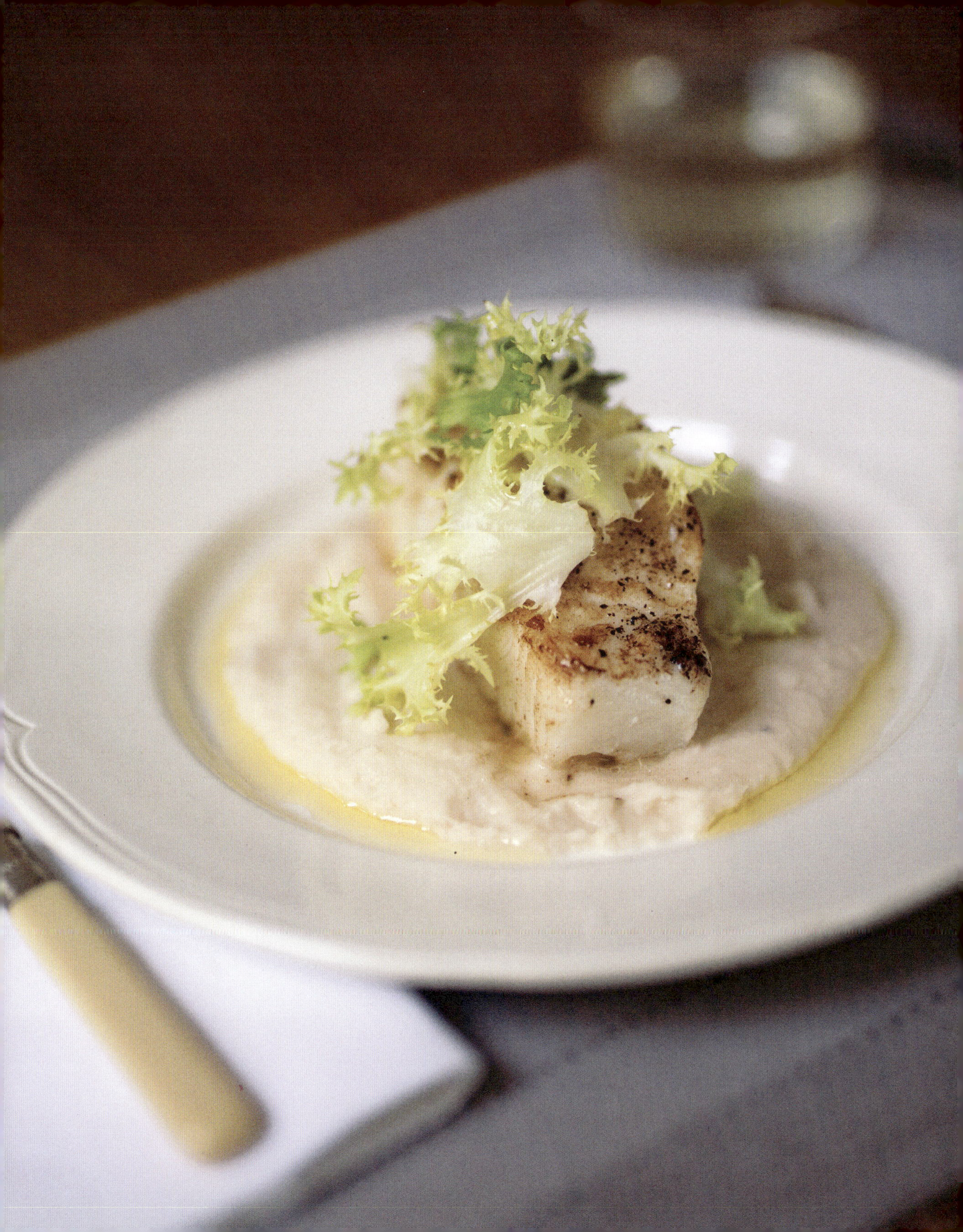

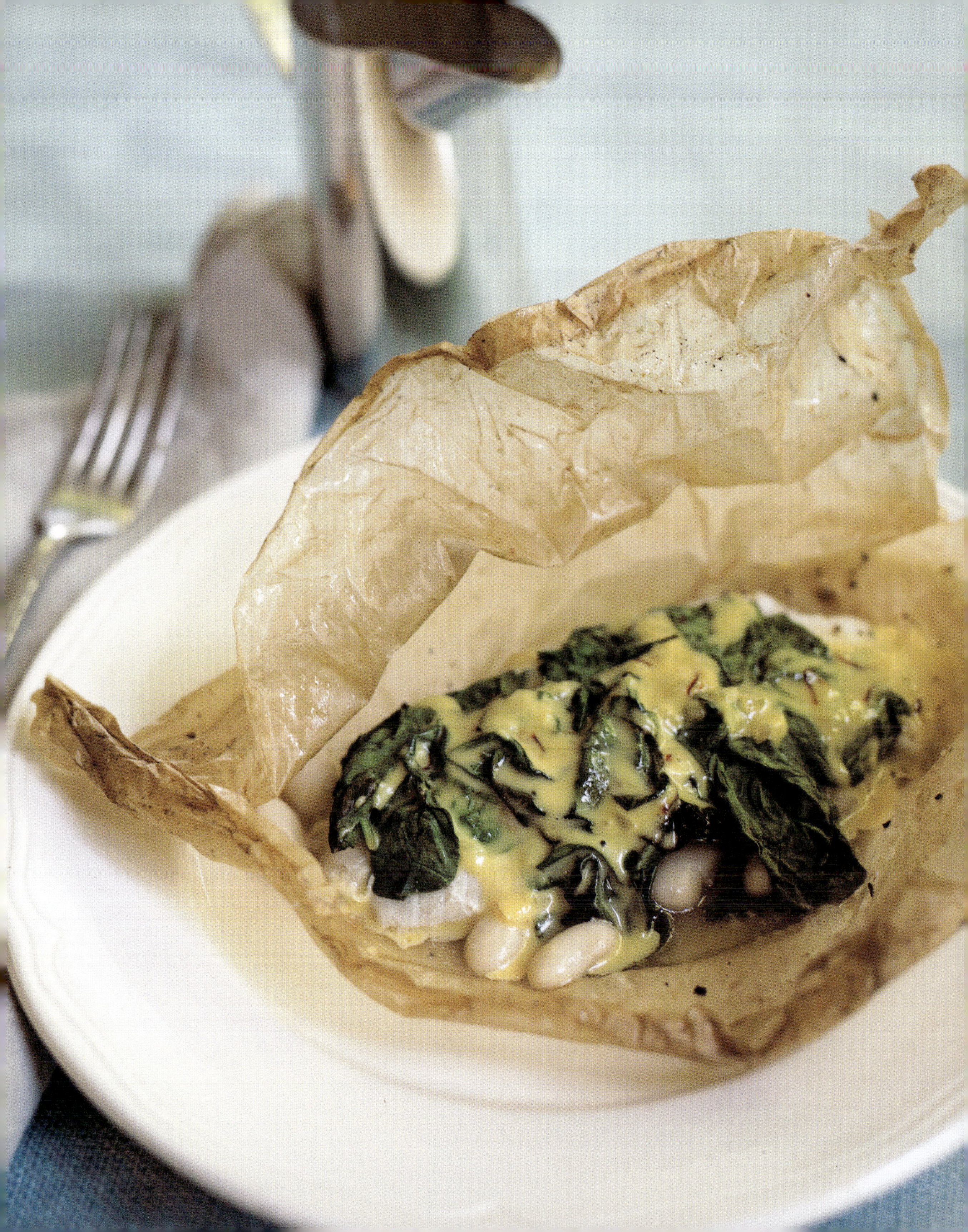

PAPILLOTES OF SOLE, WHITE BEANS, AND SPINACH *with* SAFFRON SAUCE

SERVES 4

Papillotes — half-hearts of sealed parchment packets surrounding a fish fillet, along with vegetables, herbs and seasonings — are a classic French culinary technique. They are somehow both sophisticated and simple, a rare combination. The fish and vegetables steam inside the packets, infused with the flavors of the other ingredients. Saffron sauce, a traditional regional accompaniment for seafood, makes an elegant finish to the dish.

FOR THE PAPILLOTES

2 tablespoons unsalted butter

1½ cups cooked Alubia Blanca, Coco, or Cannellini beans (see page 26), drained, warm or at room temperature

4 sole fillets, about 1½ pounds total

1 teaspoon sea salt

½ teaspoon freshly ground black pepper

2 cups fresh spinach

8 teaspoons white wine

FOR THE SAFFRON SAUCE

½ tablespoon unsalted butter

1 shallot, minced (about 2 tablespoons)

1 cup homemade fish or chicken broth (or low-salt commercial broth)

2 tablespoons heavy cream

Pinch of saffron

¼ teaspoon sea salt

¼ teaspoon freshly ground black pepper

Preheat oven to 450°F.

Cut four 14-inch rectangles of parchment paper and fold them in half. Draw a half-heart shape on each rectangle (with the heart's center along the fold), then cut along the lines. Open up the heart-shaped papers and lay them flat. Using a little of the butter, grease each paper on one side of the heart shape. Spoon one quarter of the beans atop the butter in each packet, sprinkle with a little salt and pepper, then lay a fillet atop the beans. Season with a little more salt and pepper, and top each stack with ½ cup of spinach. (The stack will be quite high, but the spinach reduces on cooking.) Sprinkle each stack with 2 teaspoons of wine, and dot with the remaining butter.

Fold over each packet: Starting at the top, fold the edges several times and pinch them together to seal. At the end, twist the paper together to seal completely. Using a spatula, transfer packets to a rimmed baking sheet.

Bake until fish is opaque and spinach has reduced, about 8 minutes. Remove from the oven and keep warm.

While the packets are cooking, make the sauce. In a small saucepan over medium-high heat, melt the butter. When it foams, add shallots; sauté until golden, about 2 minutes. Add broth and reduce by half. Add cream, saffron, salt, and pepper; cook, stirring, until thick and hot but not boiling, another 3 to 5 minutes.

To serve, place a packet on each of 4 plates and slit the packet open with scissors or a knife. Serve immediately with the hot saffron sauce.

GARLIC SHRIMP *with* WHITE BEANS *and* SAUCE VERTE

SERVES 4

Shrimp and beans, like tuna and beans, have a special affinity, and they're further complemented here with *sauce verte*, France's answer to Spanish *chimichurri* and *salsa verde*. Like its Iberian cousins, *sauce verte* is also based on green herbs — in this case, parsley — and gently spiced with garlic and shallots.

FOR THE SAUCE

1 cup flat-leaf parsley leaves, chopped

4 to 5 green onions, chopped (about ½ cup)

1 garlic clove, minced

2 tablespoons minced shallots

1 tablespoon lemon juice

¾ cup extra-virgin olive oil (divided use)

¼ teaspoon sea salt

FOR THE SHRIMP AND BEANS

4 cups cooked Lingot or Alubia Blanca beans (see page 26), with broth

2 tablespoons extra-virgin olive oil

2 garlic cloves, mashed and minced

1¼ pounds shrimp, peeled and deveined

Sea salt and freshly ground black pepper

To prepare the sauce, combine all ingredients except ½ cup olive oil in a blender or the bowl of a food processor; process to a thick paste. Gradually add remaining olive oil and blend to make a thick sauce. Taste and adjust seasoning, as desired. The sauce can be made a day ahead and filmed with more olive oil to maintain the bright green color.

To prepare the shrimp and beans: In a saucepan over medium heat, warm beans and their broth. In a skillet over medium-high heat, warm the olive oil. Add garlic and shrimp, sprinkle with salt and pepper, and sauté just until shrimp are pink and opaque, about 2 minutes.

Using a slotted spoon, divide beans equally among 4 dinner plates. Top with sautéed shrimp. Drizzle with a little sauce, serving the remainder on the side.

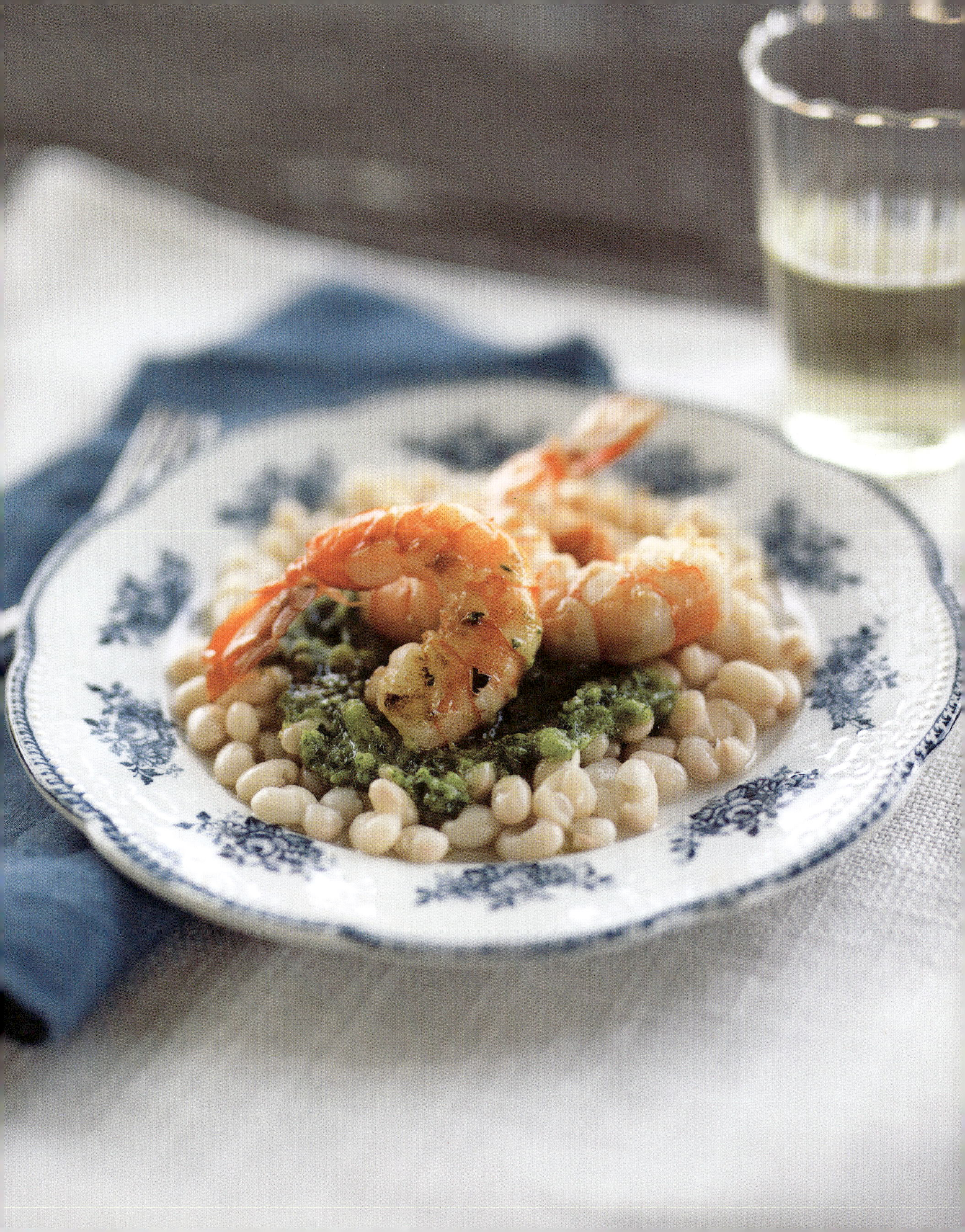

CASSOULET, MORE-OR-LESS TOULOUSE-STYLE
PAGE 98

The MYSTIQUE OF CASSOULET

Cassoulet is fundamentally a bean-and-meat farmhouse dish from southwestern France, with a crusty topping that forms during its long, slow cooking. It is traditionally made in a *cassole*, a terra-cotta baking dish that's wider at the top than the bottom. This French kitchen classic claims dozens of versions, some loaded with various preserved and fresh meats, which range from duck confit to lamb or mutton, plus assorted pork cuts, wild game, and sausage; others use only one or two meats. It's simple in its essence, yet the nuances can be infinite — and infinitely argued-over.

Cassoulet is associated primarily with three cities, memorialized in a famous saying: "Cassoulet is the God of Occitan cuisine — God in three persons. God the Father is that of Castelnaudary. God the Son is that of Carcassonne. And the Holy Spirit is that of Toulouse." Clearly, people take their cassoulet seriously. The triumvirate of cities is full of restaurants all claiming to serve the *vrai* (true) cassoulet, and delicatessens where you can get takeout cassoulet to reheat at home. Throughout southwestern France, cities and villages hold cassoulet feasts — both public and private — throughout the year, and the regional tourist bureau has even mapped out La Route du Cassoulet for gastrotourists.

The various styles of cassoulet have more commonalities than differences. Castelnaudary versions use both lamb and pork, as well as duck confit; Toulouse-style requires duck confit and garlicky local sausages; in Carcassonne, purists insist the dish must include the local red-legged partridge as well as duck confit and sausage. Some variants use tomatoes, others not. Pork skin is a key ingredient, universally.

The beans used are invariably white and locally grown. The best known is the Tarbais bean, grown in the commune of Tarbes; other notable options include the Lingot de Mazères and the Lingot de Lauragais, both cultivated an hour's drive from Carcassonne.

But cassoulet is made and served all over France, with all kinds of beans. The key is to choose beans that hold their shape during long, slow cooking and produce — when combined with the other ingredients — a flavorful broth. Beyond that, the variations are too numerous to list.

Cassoulet isn't difficult to make. It just takes time, which makes it a perfect choice for a cold winter day. The end product, even the simplest versions, always feels like a major accomplishment, especially when a crowd sits down around the table to dig beneath the bubbling crust for servings of richly flavored, slow-cooked meats and beans.

A GRAND CASSOULET with LAMB, PORK, and DUCK CONFIT

SERVES 10 TO 12

This version leans toward the tradition of the cassoulet of Castelnaudary — with the inclusion of lamb and tomatoes, as well as pork and duck confit — and finishes with a layer of fat-enriched bread crumbs that some eschew. It's more time consuming to make than some other versions, because two of the meats are individually braised before being combined with the other ingredients. It's the sort of dish that gives great pleasure to the cook, who derives almost as much enjoyment from the preparation of a dish as from the final result. If you need more fat than the confit offers, feel free to make up the difference with lard or extra-virgin olive oil.

FOR THE BEANS

3½ cups (about 1½ pounds) Tarbais, Cassoulet, or Lingot beans, soaked overnight and drained (see page 26)

1 pound lean pork belly, skin removed and reserved, meat cut into 4 pieces

1 fresh pig's foot

1 large yellow onion, peeled and studded with 5 cloves

6 garlic cloves, chopped

6 black peppercorns

3 carrots, peeled and cut into 1-inch pieces

Bouquet garni: 4 thyme sprigs, 8 flat-leaf parsley sprigs, and 2 bay leaves, tied with kitchen string

1 teaspoon sea salt

3½ quarts cold water

FOR THE MEATS

½ cup duck fat from the confit, plus more if needed (divided use)

5 Toulouse sausages (or substitute mild Italian sausage links), pricked with a toothpick in several places

5 whole confit duck legs, fat reserved, drumsticks and thighs separated

1½ to 2 pounds pork shoulder, trimmed of fat, cut into 2-inch cubes

1 teaspoon sea salt (divided use)

TO MAKE THE BEANS

In a large saucepan over medium-high heat, place the soaked beans and enough water to cover beans by about 3 inches. Bring to a boil; reduce heat to low and simmer, uncovered, until beans are soft and swollen, about 30 minutes.

In another saucepan over medium-high heat, combine pork belly, pork skin, and enough water to cover meat by about 3 inches. Bring to a boil; reduce heat to medium and cook for 20 minutes. Drain and rinse the meat and skin under running water. Cut the skin into ½-inch strips and tie with kitchen string to make little bundles.

Drain beans. In a large pot over medium-high heat, combine the beans with pork skin bundles, pork belly, pig's foot, onion, garlic, peppercorns, carrots, bouquet garni, salt, and water. Bring to a boil, then reduce heat to low. Cook, partially covered, until beans are almost but not quite tender, about 1 hour. Remove from heat and set aside.

TO PREPARE THE MEATS AND FINISH THE CASSOULET

In a large Dutch oven or casserole over medium heat, melt 2 tablespoons of the duck fat. Add sausages and cook, turning often, until browned, about 10 minutes. Remove and set aside.

Add the duck confit to the pot, skin side down. Cook, turning often, until the skin is crisp and golden, 10 to 15 minutes. Remove and set aside.

Add the cubed pork shoulder to the pot; season with ½ teaspoon salt, ½ teaspoon pepper, and 1 teaspoon thyme. Brown the meat, turning often, about 10 minutes. Remove and set aside.

Add more duck fat, if needed. Add the cubed lamb shoulder to the pot; season with remaining salt, pepper, and thyme. Brown the meat, turning often, about 10 minutes. Remove and set aside.

A GRAND CASSOULET *with* LAMB, PORK, *and* DUCK CONFIT

FOR THE MEATS (CON'T)

1 teaspoon freshly ground black pepper (divided use)

2 teaspoons fresh thyme (divided use)

2 pounds boneless lamb shoulder, cut into 2-inch cubes

2 yellow onions, minced (divided use)

12 garlic cloves, crushed (divided use)

1 pound ripe tomatoes, peeled, seeded, and finely chopped

2 tablespoons tomato paste

TO FINISH

5 thick slices country-style bread or baguette, torn into large chunks, then processed in a blender (crumbs should be chunky)

Add half of the onion and 8 garlic cloves to the pot. Sauté, stirring often, until onions are translucent, 3 or 4 minutes. Add browned pork to the pot; stir. Add the tomatoes and stir again. Add the tomato paste; stir for a minute or two, then slowly stir in 2 cups water. Reduce heat to medium-low; cover and simmer until meat is tender, about 1½ hours.

In another, smaller Dutch oven or casserole over medium-high heat, melt 1 tablespoon duck fat. Add the remaining minced onion and 4 crushed garlic cloves. Sauté until the onions are translucent, 3 or 4 minutes. Add browned lamb to the pot; stir, then slowly add 2 cups water, scraping up any clinging bits of meat. Reduce heat to medium-low; cover and simmer until meat is tender, about 1 hour.

Preheat oven to 325°F. Remove bouquet garni from the beans; discard. Remove pig's foot and onion; discard the cloves. Chop the onion and return it to the beans. Remove meat from the pig's foot and add it to the beans. Remove the pork belly from the beans, cut it into ½-inch cubes, and return them to the beans. Remove the pork-skin bundles, discard the string, and cut skin into small pieces; return them to the beans.

Remove the pork from its broth; set aside. Add the broth to the beans. Remove the lamb from its broth; set aside. Simmer the lamb broth over medium-high heat until reduced to ½ cup; add to the beans. Cut sausages into 1-inch pieces; set aside.

Rub the bottom of a large Dutch oven (or other baking dish) with some of the remaining duck fat. Using a slotted spoon, add one-third of the beans in an even layer. Cover with a layer of the mixed meats, then another layer of the beans. Cover this layer with duck confit. Top with a final layer of beans, and finish with the bread crumbs. Melt the remaining fat (about 2 tablespoons) and drizzle it over the bread crumbs. Ladle on enough of the bean broth to just cover the beans.

Place the pot in the oven and bake until a crust begins to form, about 30 minutes. With a spoon, break through the crust, scoop up some juices, and baste the crust. Repeat several more times over the next 1½ to 2 hours, adding more reserved broth as needed to keep the liquid just below the beans' surface. The final result should be slightly soupy, not dry, with a golden, crunchy crust. To serve, bring the casserole directly to the table and scoop onto dinner plates. Each serving should include a piece of duck and a few pieces of sausage.

CASSOULET, *more-or-less* TOULOUSE-STYLE

SERVES 8

My friend Kate Hill, who has lived in Gascony in the heart of southwestern France for many years, and who has written an entire book on cassoulet, taught me that sometimes less is more when it comes to packing the meats into the final dish. Preparing the beans is perhaps the most important step. Not only are you cooking the beans but you're also creating a rich, flavorful broth that will infuse the entire dish. Salting comes at the end, but you can add a little salt as the beans cook, if you'd like.

FOR THE BEANS

¼ pound fresh skin-on pork belly

Bouquet garni: 6 thyme sprigs, 6 flat-leaf parsley sprigs, and 2 bay leaves, tied with kitchen string

2 pounds Tarbais, Cassoulet, or Lingot beans, soaked overnight in cold water and drained (see page 26)

1 onion, peeled and studded with 5 cloves

¼ pound *ventriche* (or pancetta) in a whole chunk

1 large carrot, peeled and halved

2 leeks, white and light-green parts only

2 celery stalks, halved

2 garlic cloves

1 teaspoon black peppercorns

1 fresh pig's foot (optional)

½ to 1 tablespoons sea salt (divided use)

FOR THE MEATS

6 whole confit duck legs, fat reserved, drumsticks and thighs separated

5 Toulouse sausages (or substitute mild Italian sausage links), pricked with a toothpick in several places

TO PREPARE THE BEANS

Cut the pork belly crosswise into 1-inch pieces. Roll up each strip into a cylinder, tying with kitchen string.

In a large, lidded Dutch oven (or other heavy casserole), place the pork belly bundles, bouquet garni, beans, clove-studded onion, *ventriche*, carrot, leeks, celery, garlic, peppercorns, and pig's foot, if using.

Add enough water to cover beans by about 2 inches; bring to a boil over medium-high heat.

Reduce heat to low; simmer, partially covered, until beans are barely tender and broth is slightly opaque and flavorful, about 1 hour. At this point, you can add 2 teaspoons of salt. Remember, the beans will ultimately finish cooking in the oven.

TO PREPARE THE MEATS

In a skillet over medium-high heat, melt a tablespoon of reserved duck fat. Add the confit, skin side down. (If your pan is small, you may need to do this in two batches.) Cook, turning often, until the skin is crisp and golden, about 10 minutes. Remove and set aside.

Remove all but a tablespoon of the fat from the pan, reserving for later use. Add sausages, turning until they are cooked through and lightly browned, 12 to 15 minutes. Remove sausages from pan; cut each in half, reserving the fat.

CASSOULET, *more-or-less* TOULOUSE-STYLE

TO FINISH

Preheat oven to 300°F.

Remove all the meats, vegetables, and herbs from the beans. Discard the bouquet garni, cloves, and the string around the pork belly. Chop the vegetables and return them to the beans. Remove the meat from the pig's foot, discarding bones and skin. Mince the meat from the pig's foot and the pork belly; return meat to the beans.

Taste the broth and adjust seasoning, as desired. The broth should be quite flavorful, but not overly salty.

Into a wide, deep casserole or baking dish, use a slotted spoon to add enough beans to make a 1-inch layer. Top with the confit and another layer of beans. Add the sausage atop this layer, then cover with a final layer of beans. Sprinkle the top with the chopped pork belly, then ladle on enough of the bean broth to cover the beans by about ½ inch. Reserve the remaining broth for basting.

Place the casserole in the oven, uncovered. During the first hour of cooking, baste the top of the cassoulet with the reserved broth. After 1 hour of cooking, break through the crust with a wooden spoon. Repeat 2 or 3 more times, basting as needed with either the cooking liquid or the reserved broth.

Continue to bake until beans are meltingly tender, broth is bubbling along the sides, and a crispy browned crust has formed, about 2½ to 3 hours total.

To serve, bring the casserole directly to the table and scoop onto dinner plates. Each serving should include a piece of duck and sausage.

SLIGHTLY SHORT-CUT CASSOULET

SERVES 8 TO 10

This version contains fewer ingredients than the preceding two, and requires less chopping and meat-picking, yet still results in a festive, flavorful taste of southwestern France.

FOR THE BEANS

2 pounds Tarbais, Cassoulet, or Lingot beans, soaked overnight and drained (see page 26)

1 yellow onion, peeled and studded with 4 cloves

2 carrots, peeled and halved

1 celery stalk

1 ham hock (about 1½ pounds)

¼ pound chopped pancetta or bacon

4 garlic cloves, peeled

Bouquet garni: 3 thyme sprigs, 4 flat-leaf parsley sprigs, and 2 bay leaves, tied with kitchen string

1 teaspoon black peppercorns

FOR THE MEAT

5 whole confit duck legs (drumsticks and thighs), fat reserved

8 Toulouse sausages (or substitute Italian mild sausage links), pricked with a toothpick in several places

TO FINISH

1 cup canned chopped tomatoes and their juice

TO PREPARE THE BEANS

In a large pot, add beans, onion, carrots, celery, ham hock, pancetta or bacon, garlic, bouquet garni, and peppercorns, plus enough water to cover by 3 inches. Bring to a boil. Reduce heat to medium-low; cover and cook until the beans are soft but still have a bit of resistance, 1½ to 2 hours.

TO PREPARE THE MEAT AND FINISH THE CASSOULET

In a skillet over medium heat, cook duck confit in some of its fat until skin is golden, about 4 minutes per side. Remove to a cutting board. Separate drumsticks from thighs; set aside. In the same pan, cook sausages until just browned, turning often, about 10 minutes. (Do not cook all the way through; they will finish cooking with the beans.) Remove to a cutting board; cut each sausage into 3 or 4 pieces.

Preheat oven to 450°F.

Remove ham hock from the beans. Pick the meat from the bones; set meat aside, discarding skin and bones. Remove and discard the onion, carrots, and bouquet garni. With a slotted spoon, remove the beans to a bowl and set aside. Strain the bean broth into a saucepan, discarding peppercorns and any debris. Add the tomatoes and their juice; simmer to blend the flavors. Taste and adjust seasoning, as desired.

In a large Dutch oven or other casserole, add half the beans in an even layer. Top with a layer of sausages, ham, and duck confit. Cover with the remaining beans. Top with just enough broth to cover the beans, reserving the rest for basting.

Cook for 30 minutes, then reduce heat to 350°F. Continue to cook, breaking the crust and pushing it into the juices 3 or 4 times, and basting with the remaining broth if the beans appear to be drying out. Cook until the crust is deep golden and thick bubbles continue to appear around the edges, 1½ to 2 hours. To serve, bring the casserole directly to the table and scoop onto dinner plates. Each serving should include a piece of duck and a sausage.

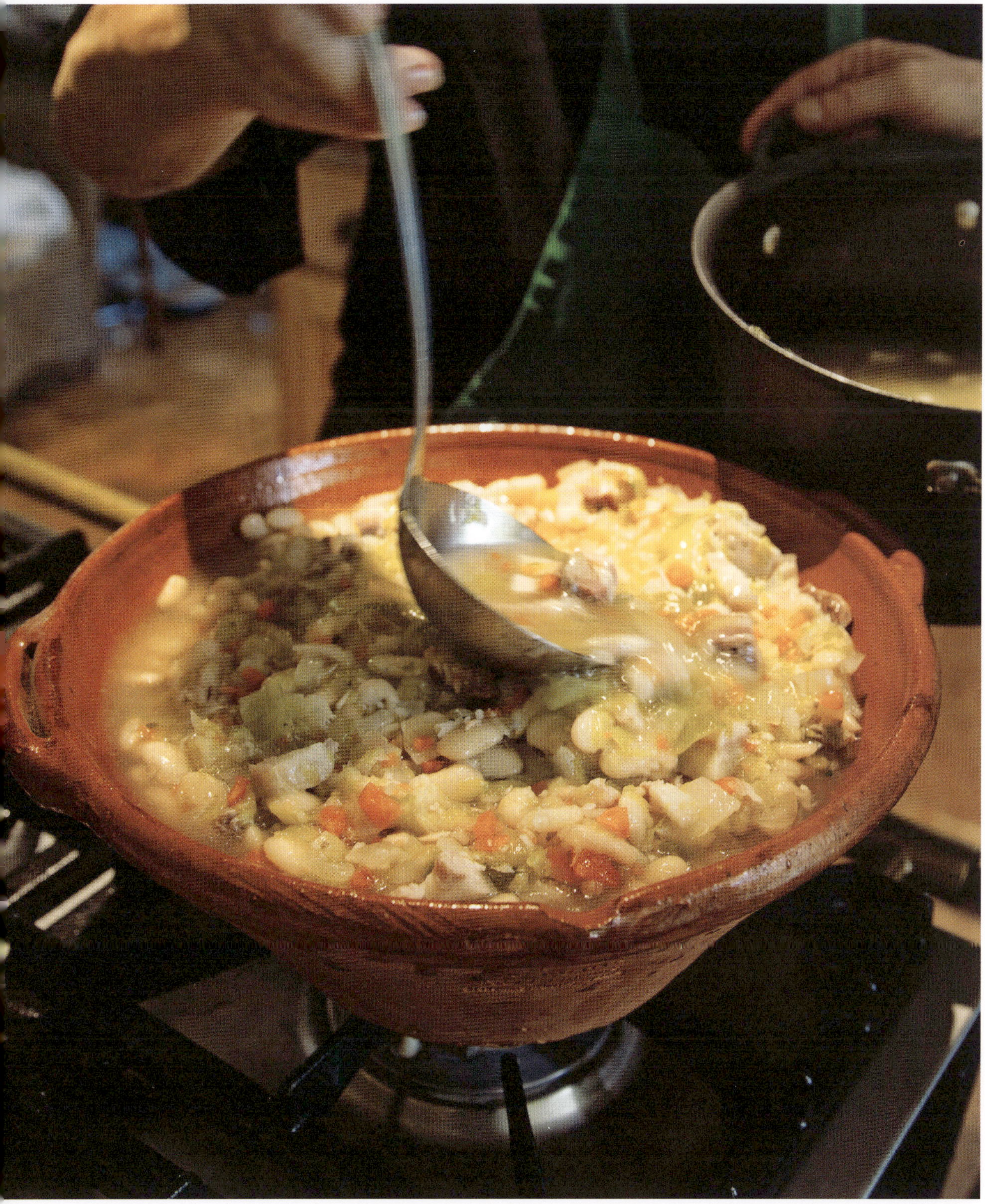

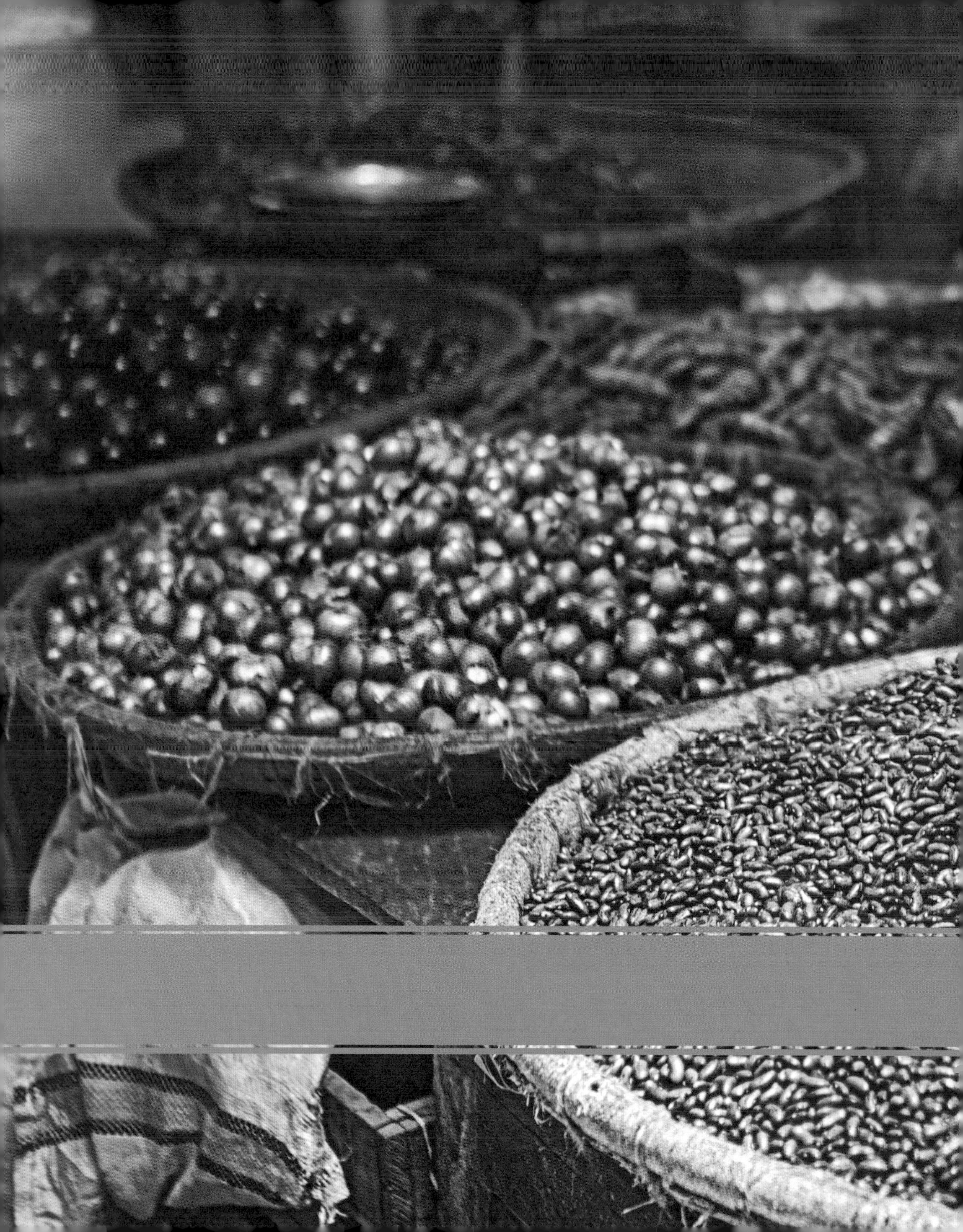

SOUPS & STEWS

CLASSIC SUMMER SOUPE AU PISTOU
PAGE 106

SOUPE AU PISTOU *and* ITS *Seasonal* VARIATIONS

Soupe au Pistou, the vegetable soup of Provence, shares many similarities with neighboring Italy's Minestrone al Pesto, but it maintains a character of its own and boasts plenty of different styles. From village to village, house to house, from Nice to St.-Rémy to Avignon, you'll find infinite variations of Soupe au Pistou. Nevertheless, all are based on the ingenuity of the frugal *provençaux* of the past who mastered using humble, seasonal vegetables from their gardens in harmony with local herbs and olive oil to create a dish that people still crave and celebrate.

Pistou is so popular that it is sometimes the centerpiece of a *fête*, a public festival, where participants gather around long tables set in the village square, with tables lined with steaming tureens of soup, piles of baguettes, and bowls of the garlic-and-basil paste known as pistou — along with local wine, of course.

The soup begins with olive oil, onions, and leeks, followed by assorted vegetables. These vary with the seasons, but shelling beans are a constant — the more the better. Coco Rouge and Coco Blanc beans, preferably both, are a basic element, with fresh green beans and carrots. Zucchini and potatoes typically feature in the familiar summer versions. From there, many differences emerge: In spring, you'll find young turnips and peas; in fall, pumpkin and sweet peppers.

Some versions include broken bits of noodles, or rice, or neither. Some have celery and celery leaves; others do not. Summer versions are more likely to have tomatoes. Feel free to experiment based on your preferences and your pantry.

In all versions, some of the pistou is stirred in at serving time, and the rest is served alongside to accompany the soup. Some claim the pistou must be made with a mortar and pestle, which I personally enjoy doing, but a blender will serve as well.

CLASSIC SUMMER
SOUPE AU PISTOU

SERVES 6

In late summer, shelling beans are just coming into season. For a short window, Coco Rouge and Coco Blanc beans are available fresh in France; when possible, these are used. When they're out of season, dried Coco beans are cooked, then added to the soup toward the end of the simmer, along with a bit of bean broth.

FOR THE PISTOU

3 or 4 garlic cloves, peeled and coarsely chopped

¼ teaspoon coarse sea salt

1 packed cup fresh basil leaves

⅓ cup extra-virgin olive oil

FOR THE SOUP

1 tablespoon extra-virgin olive oil

1 small onion, diced

2 leeks, white parts only, finely chopped

1 carrot, peeled and diced

3 small potatoes, peeled and diced

1 large zucchini, diced

3 cups homemade vegetable or chicken broth (or low-salt commercial broth)

4 cups water

1 teaspoon sea salt

½ teaspoon freshly ground black pepper

4 fresh thyme sprigs

4 fresh parsley sprigs

1 pound fresh Coco Blanc or other white beans, shelled, or 2 cups cooked (see page 26), with broth

1 pound fresh Coco Rouge or Cranberry beans, shelled, or 2 cups cooked (see page 26)

½ pound haricots verts (or other thin green beans), cut into 1-inch long pieces

½ cup broken spaghetti

FOR THE PISTOU

In a mortar, crush garlic and salt, using the pestle to make a paste. (The sharp edges of the salt crystals act like knives and help to achieve the right consistency.) Add basil leaves a few at a time, crushing each time. Finally, add olive oil in a thin stream, continuing to mix with the pestle until the mixture thickens and takes on a green tint. Set aside. (If you prefer, you can use a blender instead of the mortar and pestle.)

FOR THE SOUP

In a large saucepan or soup pot over medium-high heat, warm the olive oil. Add onion and leeks; sauté until translucent, 2 to 3 minutes. Add carrot, potatoes, and zucchini; sauté for 1 minute. Add broth, water, salt, pepper, thyme, and parsley; bring to a boil. Reduce heat to medium, cover, and cook until carrots and potatoes are tender, 20 to 25 minutes.

Add fresh Coco Blanc and Coco Rouge beans; cook another 15 minutes, or until beans are nearly tender. If you are using cooked beans, add them now, along with 2 tablespoons of bean broth. Add green beans and spaghetti; cook until pasta is tender, another 8 to 10 minutes. With the back of a fork, crush some of the potatoes and beans to thicken the soup.

Remove thyme and parsley sprigs. Taste and adjust seasoning, as desired.

Before serving, add a tablespoon of soup broth to the pistou. Pour soup into a tureen or serving bowl and stir in 2 tablespoons of pistou. Serve soup hot, with remaining pistou in a bowl on the side.

SPRINGTIME SOUPE AU PISTOU

SERVES 6

Peas and young turnips combine with traditional Soupe au Pistou ingredients to create a spring version. Here I've used Cannellini beans instead of Coco Blanc beans, and also added a little rice, because rice and peas are a classic combination.

FOR THE PISTOU

3 or 4 garlic cloves, peeled and coarsely chopped

¼ teaspoon coarse sea salt

1 packed cup fresh basil leaves

⅓ cup extra-virgin olive oil

FOR THE SOUP

1 tablespoon extra-virgin olive oil

1 small onion, diced

2 leeks, white parts only, finely chopped

2 celery stalks with leaves, chopped

1 carrot, peeled and diced

3 small potatoes, peeled and diced

3 small spring turnips, quartered

3 cups homemade vegetable or chicken broth (or low-salt commercial broth)

4 cups water

1 teaspoon sea salt

½ teaspoon freshly ground black pepper

4 fresh thyme sprigs

4 flat-leaf parsley sprigs

2 cups cooked Coco Rouge or Cranberry beans (see page 26)

2 cups cooked Coco, Lingot or Cannellini beans (see page 26), with broth

1½ pounds fresh English peas, shelled

¼ cup long grain white rice

FOR THE PISTOU

In a mortar, crush garlic and salt, using the pestle to make a paste. (The sharp edges of the salt crystals act like knives and help to achieve the right consistency.) Add basil leaves a few at a time, crushing each time. Finally, add olive oil in a thin stream, continuing to mix with the pestle until the mixture thickens and takes on a green tint. Set aside. (If you prefer, you can use a blender instead of the mortar and pestle.)

FOR THE SOUP

In a large saucepan or soup pot over medium-high heat, warm the olive oil. Add onion, leeks, celery, and celery leaves; sauté until translucent, 2 to 3 minutes. Add carrot, potatoes, and turnips; stir several times. Add broth, water, salt, pepper, thyme, and parsley; bring to a boil. Reduce heat to medium; cover and cook until carrots and potatoes are tender, 20 to 25 minutes.

Add cooked beans, 2 tablespoons of bean broth, peas, and rice. Cook until rice is tender, about 20 minutes. With the back of a fork, crush some of the potatoes and beans to thicken the soup.

To serve, remove thyme and parsley. Taste and adjust seasoning, as desired.

Before serving, add a tablespoon of soup broth to the pistou. Pour soup into a tureen or serving bowl and stir in 2 tablespoons of pistou. Serve soup hot, with remaining pistou in a bowl on the side.

FALL
SOUPE AU PISTOU
SERVES 6

Fall vegetables combine with those of late summer to make a rich, hearty soup perfect for the cooling nights of the season. Winter squash is an important element and although the ones you would find in France — usually sold in slices at the market — are the burnished copper-orange Musquée de Provence pumpkins, you can use butternut squash or any other winter squash. Sweet peppers, at their best late in the season, add both color and flavor to this version, where I've used tomatoes as well.

FOR THE PISTOU

3 or 4 garlic cloves, peeled and coarsely chopped

¼ teaspoon coarse sea salt

1 packed cup fresh basil leaves

⅓ cup extra-virgin olive oil

FOR THE SOUP

1 tablespoon extra-virgin olive oil

1 small onion, diced

2 leeks, white parts only, finely chopped

1 carrot, peeled and diced

3 small potatoes, peeled and diced

3 cups skinned, diced winter squash, such as butternut or Cinderella pumpkin

2 sweet red peppers, seeded and diced

3 cups homemade vegetable or chicken broth (or low-salt commercial broth)

2 large tomatoes, seeded and chopped, with their juice

1 teaspoon sea salt

½ teaspoon freshly ground black pepper

4 fresh thyme sprigs

4 flat-leaf parsley sprigs

1 pound fresh Coco Rouge or Cranberry beans, shelled, or 2 cups cooked (see page 26), with broth

1 pound fresh Coco Blanc or other white beans, shelled, or 2 cups cooked (see page 26), with broth

1 pound haricots verts (or other thin green beans), cut into several pieces

½ cup broken spaghetti

FOR THE PISTOU

In a mortar, crush garlic and salt, using the pestle to make a paste. (The sharp edges of the salt crystals act like knives and help to achieve the right consistency.) Add basil leaves a few at a time, crushing each time. Finally, add olive oil in a thin stream, continuing to mix with the pestle until the mixture thickens and takes on a green tint. Set aside. (If you prefer, you can use a blender instead of the mortar and pestle.)

FOR THE SOUP

In a large saucepan or soup pot over medium-high heat, warm the olive oil. Add onion and leeks; sauté until translucent, 2 to 3 minutes. Add carrot, potatoes, squash, and sweet pepper; stir several times. Add broth, 4 cups water, chopped tomatoes and their juice, salt, pepper, thyme, and parsley. Reduce heat to medium, cover and cook until carrots, potatoes, and squash are tender, 20 to 25 minutes.

Add fresh Coco Rouge and Coco Blanc beans; cook another 15 minutes, or until beans are nearly tender. If you are using cooked beans, add them now, along with 2 tablespoons of bean broth. Add green beans and spaghetti; cook until pasta is tender, another 8 to 10 minutes. With the back of a fork, crush some of the potatoes and beans to thicken the soup.

To serve, remove thyme and parsley. Taste and adjust seasoning, as desired.

Before serving, add a tablespoon of soup broth to the pistou. Pour soup into a tureen or serving bowl and stir in 2 tablespoons of pistou. Serve soup hot, with remaining pistou in a bowl on the side.

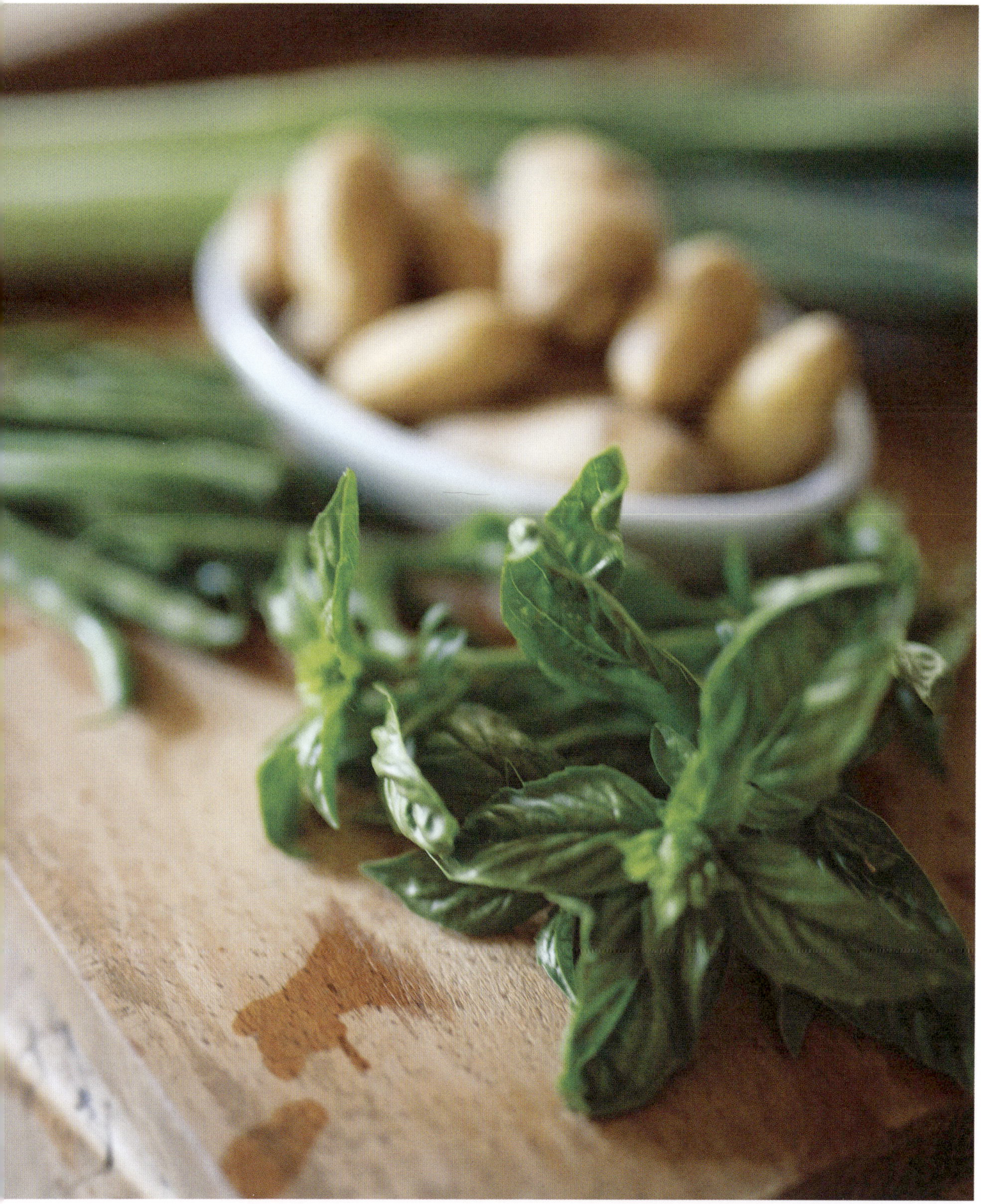

LOUBIA

SERVES 4

If you like spicy beans, you'll love *loubia*, a spicy North African dish that's also popular in France. Deep red and belly warming, it's thick with white beans, tomatoes, and aromatic vegetables, with or without meat. Like any traditional dish, *loubia* — which also means "bean" in Arabic — has multiple versions, but the flavor is defined by the array of spices. The beans are served accompanied by extra-virgin olive oil and red wine vinegar to drizzle, a finish that provides amazing results. Don't omit it. *Loubia* is a main dish stew, or it can be served, as I like to do, as accompaniment to grilled steak or lamb chops, even hamburgers.

2 tablespoons extra-virgin olive, plus more for serving

1 onion, minced

2 garlic cloves, crushed and minced

2 celery stalks with leaves, finely chopped

2 carrots, peeled and finely chopped

½ pound white beans, such as Alubia Blanca, Lingot, Tarbais, or Cassoulet, picked over and soaked (see page 26)

1 teaspoon ground cumin

1 teaspoon turmeric

1½ tablespoons paprika

1 teaspoon sea salt

1 teaspoon freshly ground black pepper

2 tablespoon tomato paste

6½ cups water

1 cup chopped canned tomatoes with juice

Red wine vinegar, for serving

In a heavy-bottomed casserole or pot over medium-high heat, warm the olive oil. Add onion and sauté until translucent, 2 or 3 minutes. Add garlic, celery, and carrots; sauté another 2 or 3 minutes. Add beans, cumin, turmeric, paprika, salt, and pepper; cook, stirring until spices are fragrant, about 1 minute. Add tomato paste; continue to stir until well incorporated, about 1 minute. Slowly add ½ cup of water, stirring to make a thin sauce. Add remaining water; bring to a boil while stirring.

Reduce heat to low, partially cover, and gently simmer for 1 hour. Add chopped tomatoes and juice, stirring well. Partially cover and continue to simmer until beans are tender, another 30 to 60 minutes, depending on the size of the beans. Check the liquid level during the last hour of cooking, adding a little more water as needed. The stew should have just enough sauce to hold it all together, but not be soupy.

In a small bowl, combine equal parts olive oil and vinegar.

To serve, spoon beans into bowls or onto dinner plates, topped with a teaspoon or more of the oil-and-vinegar condiment.

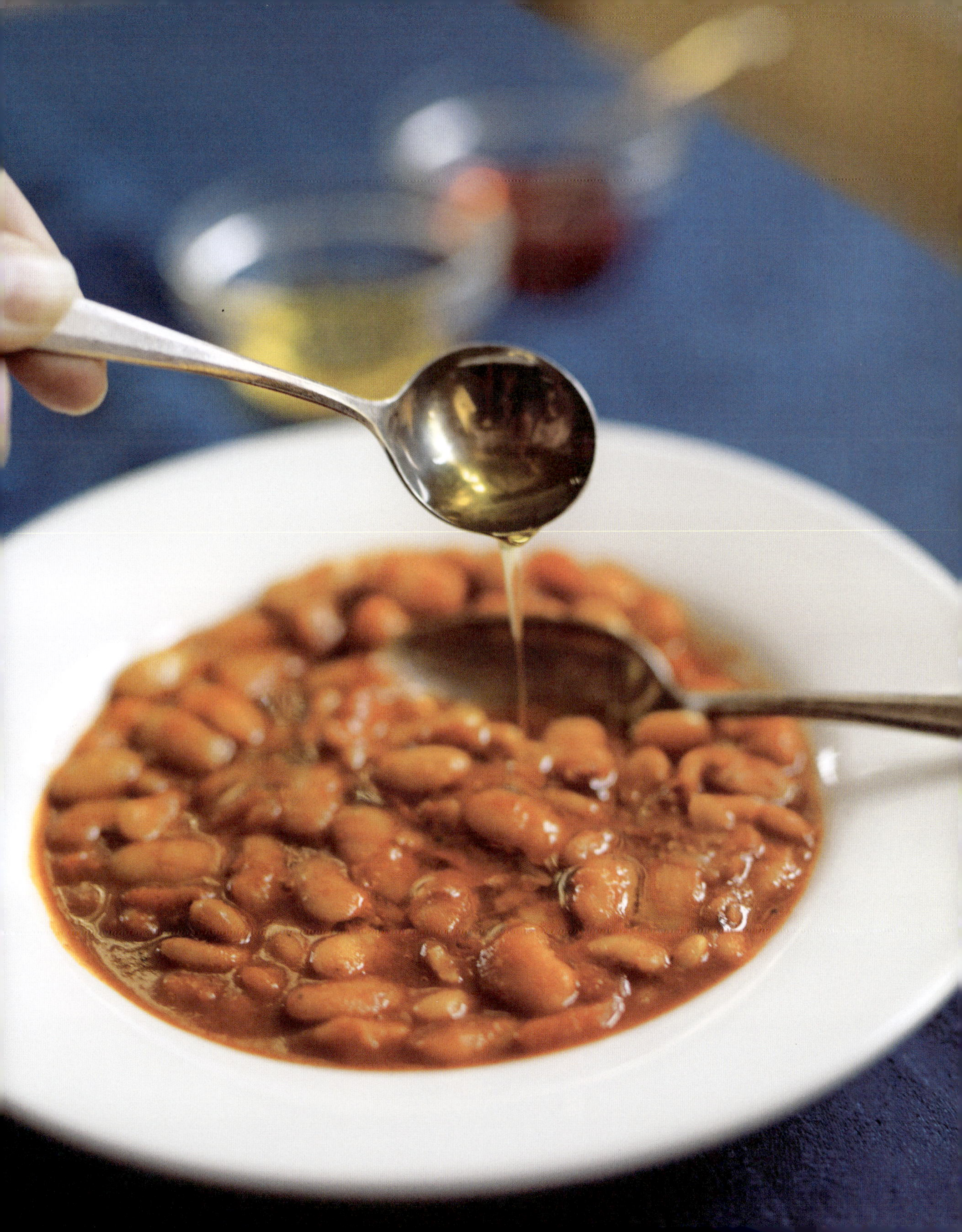

CREAM OF FENNEL and WHITE BEAN SOUP

SERVES 4

Beans are often used instead of potatoes to thicken soups, or to give flavor and texture, which is how they are used in this recipe. Adding some smoked fish elevates this soup to a special-occasion meal. Fennel is a favorite French vegetable, one we Americans sometimes overlook. It gives a mild licorice flavor, and can be eaten cooked or raw — or both, as in this soup.

2 tablespoons unsalted butter

3 large fennel bulbs, trimmed and coarsely chopped (about 6 cups), fronds minced and reserved for garnish

½ cup chopped shallots or onions

2 cups homemade chicken broth (or low-salt commercial broth)

2 cups water

1 cup cooked white beans, such as Tarbais, Cassoulet, Royal Corona, or Cannellini (see page 26), drained

4 ounces smoked trout or smoked salmon (divided use)

1 teaspoon lemon juice

½ teaspoon salt

4 tablespoons crème fraîche for garnish

In a heavy casserole over medium-high heat, melt the butter. When it foams, add chopped fennel and shallots. Sauté until shallots are translucent, about 10 minutes. Add broth and water; bring to a boil, then reduce heat to low. Cover and simmer until vegetables are soft, about 35 minutes. During the last 10 minutes of cooking, add the beans and 2 tablespoons of smoked fish, reserving the rest for garnish. Remove from heat; stir in lemon juice and salt. Taste and adjust seasoning, as desired.

Purée the mixture in a blender, then strain through a fine sieve into a clean pot over medium-low heat. Warm the purée to serving temperature, being careful not to boil.

Ladle into 4 soup bowls. Top each serving with a tablespoon of crème fraîche, a teaspoon of smoked fish, and a sprinkle of fennel fronds. Serve immediately.

RAGOUT *of* CHICKPEAS *and* CHORIZO

SERVES 4 TO 6

Spanish chorizo is one of those ingredients — like other cured meats, olives, and capers — that brings multiple flavors to a dish. When using these complex characters, you need only a few other elements to achieve a satisfying, deeply flavored dish, like this one based on chickpeas.

¾ to 1 pound Spanish-style chorizo

3 tablespoons extra-virgin olive oil

½ cup minced shallots

3 tablespoons tomato paste

½ teaspoon sugar

1 teaspoon dried oregano

½ teaspoon sea salt

½ teaspoon freshly ground black pepper

2 cups chickpea broth (or a combination of broth and water)

½ pound cooked chickpeas (see page 26)

Pinch of saffron (optional)

Slit the casing of the chorizo with a sharp knife; peel casing away and discard. Slice chorizo into ½-inch rounds, and then cut each round in half. Set aside.

In a Dutch oven over medium-high heat, warm the olive oil. Add shallots and sauté until translucent, about 2 minutes.

With a slotted spoon, remove shallots to a bowl and set aside. Add chorizo to the pan; reduce heat to medium and sauté until chorizo gleams, about 2 minutes. Return shallots to the pan; add tomato paste, sugar, oregano, salt, and pepper; stir well. Slowly add broth, mixing with the tomato mixture and scraping up any clinging bits of meat to make a light sauce.

Add cooked chickpeas and saffron, if desired. Reduce heat to medium-low; partially cover and cook until flavors are well blended, about 20 minutes. Taste and adjust seasoning, as desired. To serve, ladle into bowls.

COUSCOUS GARNI

SERVES 6 TO 8

Couscous is a tiny semolina pasta of North African origin, with nearly 1,000 years of history. Traditionally hand-rolled and then sun-dried, modern couscous is produced commercially on a large scale. It comes in several sizes: fine, medium, and large, the latter of which is sometimes called Israeli couscous.

Couscous has been firmly embraced by the French, and today it is considered one of their national dishes. The prepared dish, *couscous garni* — with garnishes that include chickpeas, vegetables, broth, and meats — can be found in restaurants, homes, and markets all over France. In the open-air markets, vendors stir steaming pots of vegetables and broth with one spoon, chicken or lamb with another, all while tending to a grill piled with spicy merguez sausage — one of the favorite *garnies*. It's French takeout food.

The customer decides the size — a serving for four, six, or eight people — and the vendor scoops an appropriate amount of steamy-hot couscous into one *barquette* (box) and the garni of vegetables and broth into another, along with the meat of choice. The whole kit is meant to be taken home and eaten accompanied by harissa, the North African chile sauce that — along with the chickpeas — is considered an essential part of the dish.

Harissa comes in tubes that can be bought in specialty markets or by mail order. Merguez can be difficult to find, but you can substitute grilled lamb chops or chicken, or another spicy sausage like andouille.

FOR THE VEGETABLES

2 tablespoons unsalted butter

2 tablespoons extra-virgin olive oil

2 onions, chopped

2 garlic cloves, chopped

½ teaspoon kosher salt or sea salt

½ teaspoon freshly ground black pepper

1 teaspoon fresh thyme leaves (or ½ teaspoon dried thyme)

4 carrots, peeled and cut into ½-inch pieces

3 young turnips, peeled and cut into ½-inch pieces

2 cups homemade chicken or vegetable broth (or low salt commercial broth)

2 zucchini, cut into ½-inch cubes or rounds

½ pound green beans, cut into 1-inch pieces

2 cups cooked chickpeas (see page 26), drained

Harissa, to taste

In a Dutch oven over medium heat, melt butter with olive oil. When the mixture foams, add onions and garlic; sauté until onion is translucent, 3 to 4 minutes. Add salt, pepper, and thyme, then carrots and turnips, turning vegetables gently in the butter mixture for 1 to 2 minutes. Pour broth over the vegetables and stir for another 1 to 2 minutes. Cover and reduce heat to low. Cook 10 minutes, then add zucchini; continue to cook until all vegetables are tender when pierced with the tip of a knife, about another 15 minutes.

Add green beans and cooked chickpeas; cover and cook until green beans are tender, another 10 minutes. Add a teaspoon or more of harissa to the vegetable broth, according to your preference for spiciness.

About 10 minutes before the vegetables are done, place a saucepan over high heat. Add boiling water and salt; bring back to a boil. Add couscous and turn off the heat. Remove the pan from the heat, cover, and let stand 10 minutes. Add the butter and gently toss the couscous with a fork until all the grains are separate and fluffy.

COUSCOUS GARNI

FOR THE COUSCOUS

2 cups boiling water

½ teaspoon sea salt

10 ounces fine couscous

1 tablespoon unsalted butter

TO FINISH

12 to 16 merguez sausages, grilled or broiled

¼ cup harissa

To serve, mound couscous on one platter, sausage on another. Put vegetables and their broth in a serving bowl and fill a small bowl with harissa to serve on the side. Serve hot.

CARBONNADE with LINGOT DU NORD BEANS

SERVES 4 TO 6

In the region of Pas-de-Calais in northern France near the Belgian border, one of the most traditional of dishes is *carbonnade*, a stew of sinewy beef slowly simmered in local dark beer along with onions, brown sugar, and — most curiously — slices of *pain d'épices*, a sturdy, cake-like bread made with dark rye flour and honey, spiced with cinnamon, ginger, black pepper, and nutmeg. Before going into the stew, the slices are spread with mustard. I know this sounds strange, but they cook down over time, and serve to both thicken and season the sauce. *Pain de campagne* or other country-style bread can be used instead; in that case, a little more brown sugar should be added to the mix. The *pain d'épices* will dissolve into the stew, but *pain de campagne* will float. It can either be crushed into the stew during the final hour of cooking, or left on top, rather like French onion soup.

The Lingot du Nord bean has been grown in northern France since the 1800s and is as highly prized as carbonnade. Traditionally, the stew is served with potatoes — steamed, mashed, or fried — but these beans make for both an apt regional pairing and an agreeable change from the usual potato.

2½ to 3 pounds of boneless beef shank, beef cheek, or beef chuck, trimmed and cut into 1½- to 2-inch cubes

1 teaspoon sea salt

½ teaspoon freshly ground black pepper

3 bacon slices, cut into ½-inch pieces

4 tablespoons lard or unsalted butter (divided use)

2 yellow onions, thinly sliced

3 to 4 tablespoons brown sugar (divided use)

3 fresh thyme sprigs

2 bay leaves

1½ tablespoons flour

2⅔ cups beer, preferably dark ale

5 thin slices pain d'épices or pain de campagne (or other country-style bread)

2½ tablespoons Dijon mustard

1 to 2 cups homemade beef broth (or low-salt commercial broth)

½ pound cooked Lingot du Nord, Mogette de Vendée, or Cannellini beans (see page 26), with broth

Preheat oven to 325°F. Sprinkle beef with salt and pepper, and set aside.

In a Dutch oven or heavy ovenproof casserole over medium-high heat, render bacon until crisp. Remove bacon and save for another use. Add 2 tablespoons of lard or butter to bacon fat; when it is hot, add meat in batches. Brown meat, turning once or twice, then remove to a bowl. Continue until all meat is browned.

Add remaining 2 tablespoons of lard or butter and onions, sautéing until they start to turn golden, about 4 minutes. Sprinkle onions with 2 tablespoons of brown sugar, and stir several times. Add thyme, bay leaves, and any remaining salt and pepper. Return meat and any collected juices to the pot; stir to coat the meat with the onions. Sprinkle with flour and stir until flour browns. Add a little beer, scraping up any clinging bits of meat. Gradually add the rest of the beer and reduce heat to low.

Spread each slice of bread with ½ tablespoon of mustard. Lay the prepared bread on top of the stew, cover the pot and place in the preheated oven. After about 45 minutes of cooking, the beer will have reduced somewhat. Add about ½ cup of beef broth now, and another ½ cup (or more) broth after another 45 minutes. The sauce should thicken, but enough liquid should remain to finish cooking the meat until it's fork tender, 2½ to 3½ hours total. During the last half hour of cooking, taste and adjust seasoning, and crush the bread into the stew, if desired.

When the stew is almost ready, reheat the beans. To serve, spoon some beans onto a dinner plate and spoon some meat and sauce over them.

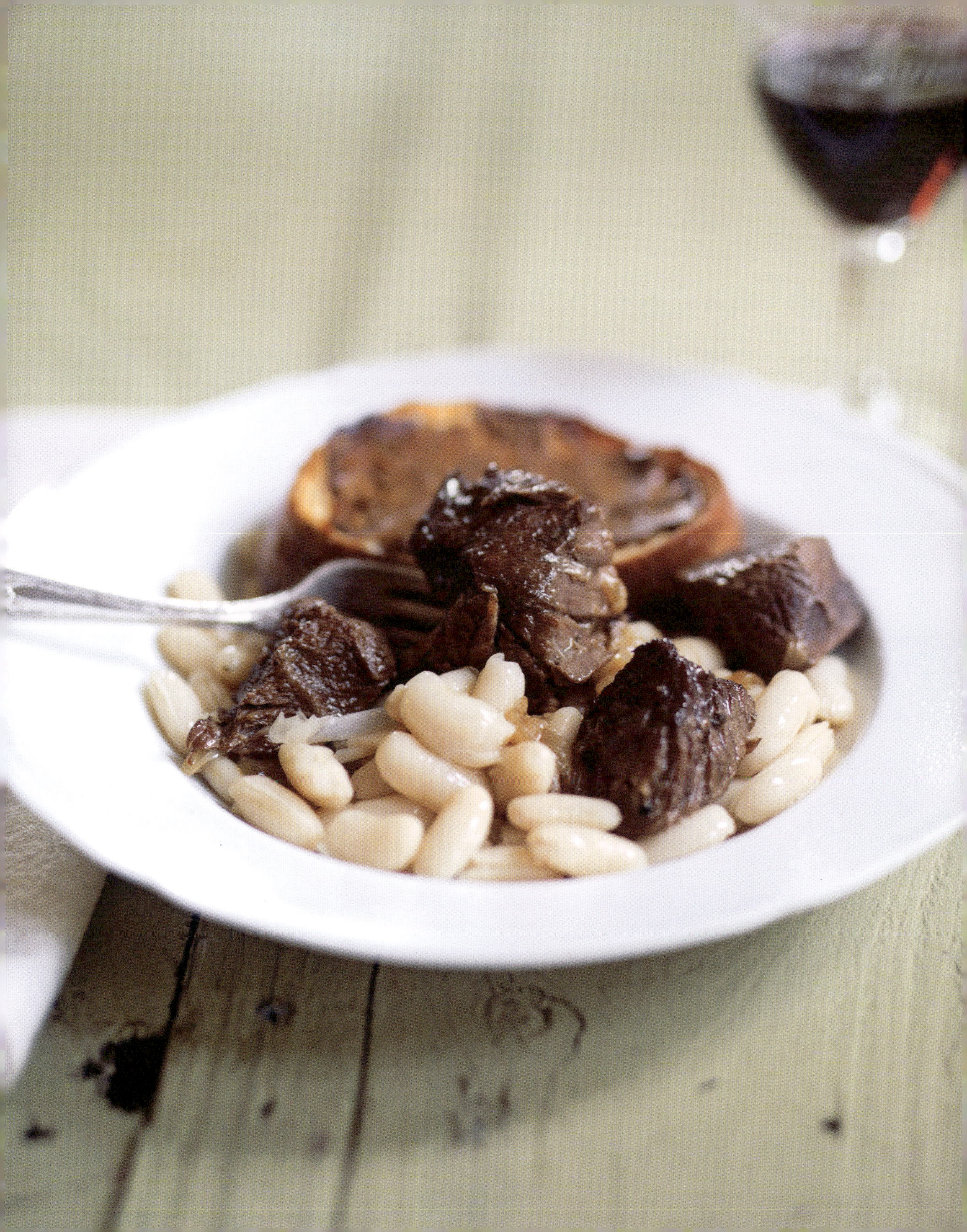

GARBURE

SERVES 6 TO 8

Garbure is a rib-sticking soup of vegetables, beans, and meat that's traditional in the Béarn region of the Pyrenees mountains in southwestern France. Garbure is so popular that, every year on the first weekend of September, the city of Oleron-Sainte-Marie holds a *garburade* — a contest to see who makes the best garbure. The winner is designated the world champion.

As always with traditional dishes, there are multiple claims to authenticity. In general, however, the beans used are Tarbais or the even-more-local Haricot de Maïs, which are slightly smaller. Traditional vegetables depend on what is in season, but usually feature cabbage, carrots, onions, and potatoes. In the Béarn, favored meats include a shank end of a salt-cured Bayonne ham — or at least a good chunk of one — and, for the finer versions, a duck carcass and wings, or thighs of duck confit. For some, the soup must be thick enough for a wooden spoon to stand straight up. In other versions, the broth is ladled over a thick piece of country-style bread and served as a first course, with the vegetables, beans, and meat served as a separate main dish, accompanied by cornichons and more bread.

Like most soups and stews, this is one of those dishes that is even better the next day or the day after.

4 quarts water

1 shank end of Bayonne or other salt-cured ham, or smoked ham hock (about 1½ pounds)

½ pound pancetta, cut into large chunks, or 1 fresh pork trotter

6 peppercorns

4 duck confit thighs with fat

2 onions, chopped

2 leeks, white parts only, thinly sliced

4 garlic cloves, chopped

1 pound Tarbais, Cassoulet, Lingot or other medium white bean, picked over and soaked (see page 26)

4 potatoes, about ½ pound

4 carrots, peeled and cut into ½-inch pieces

1 large or 2 small turnips, peeled and cut into ½-inch pieces

1 head Savoy or other green cabbage, cored and cut lengthwise into 1-inch strips

6 slices country-style bread, slightly stale

In a large stockpot over medium-high heat, combine water, ham, pancetta or trotter, and peppercorns; bring to a boil.

In a skillet over medium heat, cook the duck confit, turning from time to time until the skin is crisp and the fat melts. Remove duck from the pan; pour off all but 3 tablespoons of fat and reserve for another use. Add onions, leeks, and garlic to the remaining duck fat; sauté just until soft, 3 to 4 minutes. Using a slotted spoon, add vegetables to the simmering pot with the ham, then add beans to the pot.

Reduce heat to medium-low, partially cover, and simmer, skimming foam from time to time. When beans are nearly done and meat is beginning to fall off the bone (about 1½ hours), remove meat to a plate. Add potatoes, carrots, turnips, and cabbage to the soup along with reserved duck. Simmer until vegetables are tender and soup is quite thick, 20 to 30 minutes. Remove duck from the soup. Pick ham and duck meat from the bones and shred it using two forks. Discard skin and bones; set meat aside.

To serve, place a piece of bread in each of 6 soup bowls. Ladle some hot broth over the bread for the first course. While enjoying the first course, add the shredded meat to the soup and warm through. Spoon vegetables, meat, and beans into a serving bowl, and ladle some broth over them. This is the second course. Serve any remaining broth alongside.

Alternatively, you can omit the first course, add the shredded meat to the soup, and serve directly into soup bowls.

BRETON BEANS

SERVES 4 TO 6

This simple but flavorful dish comes from the recipe collection of Steve Sando. It's a tribute to his best friend's mother, a Russian immigrant who grew up in Brittany, on the west coast of France — the only area where the famous Coco de Paimpol bean is grown. Although the specifics are lost to history, I suspect Cocos might have been the beans she used to make this dish. The original recipe insists that that "the beans must be from the most recent harvest, so a 2-hour soak in cold water is sufficient."

½ pound white beans, such as Coco de Paimpol or other round white beans, or Lingot or Cannellini beans, picked over and soaked (see page 26)

1 teaspoon sea salt (divided use)

2 onions (divided use)

1 clove

4 garlic cloves (divided use)

½ of a carrot, peeled

Bouquet garni: 1 thyme sprig, 2 flat-leaf parsley sprigs, and ½ of a bay leaf, tied with kitchen string

2 tablespoons unsalted butter (divided use)

½ cup dry white wine

1 tomato, peeled, seeded, and chopped, with its juice

½ teaspoon freshly ground black pepper

Cover beans with cold water and soak for 2 hours.

In a saucepan over medium-high heat, add beans and enough cold water to cover beans by about 2 inches. Bring to a boil and cook for 10 minutes, then drain. Return beans to the saucepan, cover yet again with cold water, and add ½ teaspoon salt. Stud 1 onion with the clove and add it to the beans along with 2 garlic cloves, carrot, and the bouquet garni. Return the saucepan to medium-high heat, bring water to a boil; cook for 10 minutes, skimming off any foam. Reduce heat to low; simmer until beans are tender, about 1 to 1½ hours.

While the beans are cooking, prepare the other ingredients: Mince the remaining onion. In a saucepan large enough to eventually hold the beans, over medium-high heat, melt 1 tablespoon butter. When it foams, add minced onion; sauté until onion starts to turn golden, 3 to 4 minutes. While stirring, add white wine and the tomato and its juice. Grate two remaining garlic cloves; add to the saucepan along with the pepper and the remaining ½ teaspoon of salt. Reduce heat to low; stir, cooking until flavors blend and the mixture is thickened, about 15 minutes.

Drain cooked beans, discarding the clove-studded onion, carrot, and bouquet garni. Add the beans to the tomato-onion mixture; stir to combine. Remove from heat and gently stir in remaining 1 tablespoon butter. Serve hot, ladled into bowls.

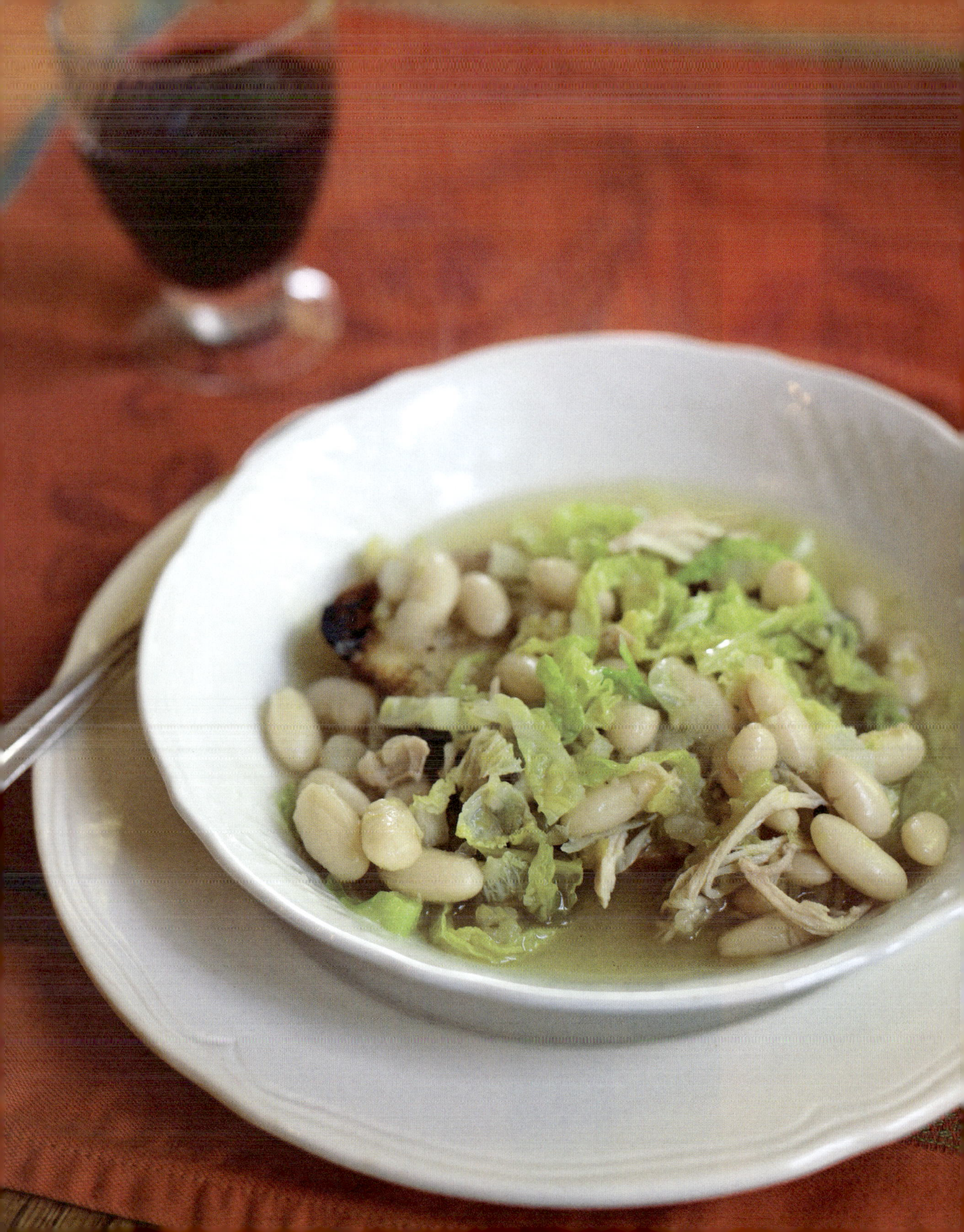

PÉRIGORD-STYLE DUCK SOUP *with* WHITE BEANS

SERVES 6

This is a grand example of the French knack for thrifty, creative country cooking. In southwest France — foie gras country — duck is common fare. Legs and wings are treated to a slow simmer in duck fat to make confit; duck pâtés and terrines abound, and duck breasts are a perennial favorite. Carcasses are turned into well-seasoned soups, sometimes called by the inelegant name *Soupe au Carcasse*, replete with seasonal vegetables and beans. When the soup bowls are almost empty, a robust slug of red table wine is poured into each bowl to make the traditional finish known as the *chabrot*, which is slurped from the bowl.

2 tablespoons duck fat (or lard or unsalted butter)

1 duck carcass (or turkey, goose, or chicken carcass)

3 carrots, peeled and diced

2 leeks, white and light-green parts only, finely chopped

2 onions, diced

3 garlic cloves, crushed and minced

1 cup water, plus more for beans

Bouquet garni: 2 thyme sprigs, 2 parsley sprigs, and 1 bay leaf, tied with kitchen string

½ pound Tarbais, Cassoulet, Lingot, Cannellini, or other medium white beans, picked over and rinsed

½ teaspoon freshly ground black pepper

½ to 1 teaspoon sea salt

1 small Savoy cabbage, cored, halved, and cut into ½-inch slices

Country-style bread, sliced, grilled or lightly toasted

Dry red wine (optional)

In a large Dutch oven over medium-high heat, melt the duck fat. Add the carcass and brown, turning often, about 5 to 7 minutes. Remove carcass to a plate. Add carrots, leeks, onions, and garlic to the pot. Sauté until onions and leeks are translucent, about 3 minutes. Add water, scraping up any clinging bits of meat, then add the bouquet garni and beans. Return the carcass and any collected juices to the pot with enough water to cover beans by about 3 inches; add pepper. Bring to a boil, skimming off any foam, then reduce heat to low and simmer, partially covered, for 1 hour. Add salt and cabbage. Continue to cook until beans are tender, about another 1 to 1½ hours.

Remove the carcass. Pick all meat from the bones, chopping any large chunks into bite-size pieces. Return meat to the pot and discard the bones. Taste the broth and adjust seasoning, as desired.

To serve, place a piece of grilled bread in each of 6 bowls and ladle soup over bread. Accompany with additional bread.

When bowls are nearly empty and diners are sated with soup, add a half-glass of red wine to each bowl, to spoon or to slurp.

INDEX

A

Alubia Blanca beans
  about, 17, *16*
  Basque-Style Beans with Standing Pork Rib Roast, 84–85, *85*
  Buttered Garlic Toasts with White Beans and Crispy Pork, 32, *33*
  Creamy White Bean and Anchovy Dip, 40, *41*
  Loubia, 110, *111*
  Papillotes of Sole, White Beans, and Spinach with Saffron Sauce, *90*, 91
  Smoked Salmon and White Bean Rillettes, 42
  White Beans with Lardons, Red Peppers, and Piment d'Espelette, 56
Anchovies
  Classic Salade Niçoise, 52
  Creamy White Bean and Anchovy Dip, 40, *41*
  in Salade Niçoise, 49
Andrieux, M., 10
AOC (Appellation d'Origine Contrôlée), 25
AOP (Appellation d'Origine Protégée), 25
Appetizers. *see* Spreads, dips, and appetizers
Arugula
  Grilled Calamari with Coco Beans and Charred Tomatoes, *64*, 65
  Salad of Salt Cod and White Beans, 57
  White Beans with Arugula, Prosciutto, and Parmesan Vinaigrette, *58*, 59
  White Beans with Lardons, Red Peppers, and Piment d'Espelette, 56
Avocados
  Salade Mexicaine, 62, *63*

B

Bacon
  Carbonnade with Lingot du Nord Beans, 116, *117*
  Slightly Short-Cut Cassoulet, 100, *101*
  White Beans with Lardons, Red Peppers, and Piment d'Espelette, 56
Basil
  Braised Chicken Thighs with Cranberry Beans and Basil, 83
  Classic Summer Soupe au Pistou, *104*, 106
  Fall Soupe au Pistou, 108, *109*
  Springtime Soupe au Pistou, 107
Basque-Style Beans with Standing Pork Rib Roast, 84–85, *85*
Bass
  Sea Bass on a Bed of Puréed White Beans, 88, *89*
Beans. *see also specific beans*
  cooking dried beans, 26, *27*
  history, 10–11
  profiles, 12–21
Beef
  Carbonnade with Lingot du Nord Beans, 116, *117*
  Hachis Parmentier, 79
  Rosemary White Beans with Beef and Cherry Tomato Brochettes, *86*, 87
Beer
  Carbonnade with Lingot du Nord Beans, 116, *117*
Beignets, Chickpea, *44*, 45
Bell peppers. *see also* Red peppers
  Classic Salade Niçoise, 52
  Gratin of Cranberry Beans, Sweet Peppers, and Toulouse Sausage, *80*, 81
  Salade Niçoise with Cranberry Beans and Tuna Confit, 50
Black beans
  Black Bean Hummus, 34
  Salade Mexicaine, 62, *63*
Black olives
  Chickpeas with Prosciutto, Black Olives, and Cherry Tomatoes, 66, *67*
  Classic Salade Niçoise, 52, *53*
  Salade Niçoise with Cranberry Beans and Tuna Confit, 50
  Salade Niçoise with Seared Tuna and White Beans, *48*, 51
Borlotti beans. *see* Coco Rouge beans
Braised Chicken Thighs with Cranberry Beans and Basil, 83
Bread
  Carbonnade with Lingot du Nord Beans, 116, *117*
  Garbure, 118
  Périgord-Style Duck Soup with White Beans, *120*, 121
Breton Beans, 119
Brochettes, Rosemary White Beans with Beef and Cherry Tomato, *86*, 87
Butter lettuce
  Classic Salade Niçoise, 52
Buttered Garlic Toasts with White Beans and Crispy Pork, 32, *33*

C

Cabbage
  Garbure, 118
  Périgord-Style Duck Soup with White Beans, *120*, 121
Calamari, Grilled, with Coco Beans and Charred Tomatoes, *64*, 65
Cannellini beans
  Basque-Style Beans with Standing Pork Rib Roast, 84–85, *85*
  Breton Beans, 119
  Buttered Garlic Toasts with White Beans and Crispy Pork, 32, *33*
  Carbonnade with Lingot du Nord Beans, 116, *117*
  Cream of Fennel and White Bean Soup, 112
  Creamy White Bean and Anchovy Dip, 40, *41*
  Gratin of Leeks and White Beans with Gruyère, 78
  Grilled Calamari with Coco Beans and Charred Tomatoes, *64*, 65
  Papillotes of Sole, White Beans, and Spinach with Saffron Sauce, *90*, 91
  Périgord-Style Duck Soup with White Beans, *120*, 121
  Rosemary White Beans with Beef and Cherry Tomato Brochettes, *86*, 87
  Salade Niçoise with Seared Tuna and White Beans, *48*, 51
  Smoked Salmon and White Bean Rillettes, 42
  Smoked Trout, Shaved Celery, and White Beans with Tarragon Vinaigrette, 61
  Springtime Soupe au Pistou, 107
  White Bean and Chorizo Tartines, *36*, 37
  White Bean, Watercress, and Pickled Herring Salad, 54, *55*
  White Beans with Lardons, Red Peppers, and Piment d'Espelette, 56
Carbonnade with Lingot du Nord Beans, 116, *117*
Cassoulet, 94–101
  about, 95

Cassoulet, More-or-Less Toulouse-Style, 94, 98–99, *99*
A Grand Cassoulet with Lamb, Pork, and Duck Confit, 96–97
mystique of, 95
Slightly Short-Cut Cassoulet, 100, *101*
Cassoulet beans. see also Tarbais beans; White beans
 about, 14
 Basque-Style Beans with Standing Pork Rib Roast, 84–85, *85*
 Cassoulet, More-or-Less Toulouse-Style, 94, 98–99, *99*
 Cream of Fennel and White Bean Soup, 112
 Garbure, 118
 A Grand Cassoulet with Lamb, Pork, and Duck Confit, 96–97
 Hachis Parmentier, 79
 Loubia, 110, *111*
 Périgord-Style Duck Soup with White Beans, *120*, 121
 Salade Niçoise with Seared Tuna and White Beans, *48*, 51
 Sea Bass on a Bed of Puréed White Beans, 88, *89*
 Slightly Short-Cut Cassoulet, 100, *101*
 Smoked Trout, Shaved Celery, and White Beans with Tarragon Vinaigrette, 61
 White Bean And Chorizo Tartines, *36*, 37
 White Bean, Watercress, and Pickled Herring Salad, 54, *55*
Cherry tomatoes. see Tomatoes
Chevrier, Gabriel, 13
Chicken
 Braised Chicken Thighs with Cranberry Beans and Basil, 83
 Périgord-Style Duck Soup with White Beans, *120*, 121
Chickpeas
 about, 18, *19*
 Chickpea and Lamb Gratin with Harissa, 82
 Chickpea Beignets, *44*, 45
 Chickpeas with Prosciutto, Black Olives, and Cherry Tomatoes, 66, *67*
 Couscous Garni, 114–115, *115*
 Fried Panisse Batons, 38
 Ragout of Chickpeas and Chorizo, 113
 Spicy Roasted Chickpeas, 39

Chorizo
 Ragout of Chickpeas and Chorizo, 113
 White Bean And Chorizo Tartines, *36*, 37
Cilantro
 Chickpea Beignets, *44*, 45
 Salade Mexicaine, 62, *63*
Classic Salade Niçoise, 52
Classic Summer Soupe au Pistou, *104*, 106
Coco beans
 about, 14
 Grilled Calamari with Coco Beans and Charred Tomatoes, *64*, 65
 Papillotes of Sole, White Beans, and Spinach with Saffron Sauce, *90*, 91
 Springtime Soupe au Pistou, 107
 White Beans with Lardons, Red Peppers, and Piment d'Espelette, 56
Coco Blanc beans
 about, 14
 Classic Summer Soupe au Pistou, *104*, 106
 Fall Soupe au Pistou, 108, 109
 Salade Niçoise with Seared Tuna and White Beans, *48*, 51
Coco de Paimpol beans
 about, 14
 Breton Beans, 119
Coco de Pamiers beans, 17
Coco Rouge beans
 about, 17
 Classic Summer Soupe au Pistou, *104*, 106
 Fall Soupe au Pistou, 108, *109*
 Springtime Soupe au Pistou, 107
Cod. see Salt cod
Corn
 Salade Mexicaine, 62, *63*
Couscous Garni, 114–115, *115*
Cranberry beans
 Braised Chicken Thighs with Cranberry Beans and Basil, 83
 Classic Summer Soupe au Pistou, *104*, 106
 Fall Soupe au Pistou, 108, *109*
 Gratin of Cranberry Beans, Sweet Peppers, and Toulouse Sausage, *80*, 81
 Salade Niçoise with Cranberry Beans and Tuna Confit, 50
 Springtime Soupe au Pistou, 107
Cream of Fennel and White Bean Soup, 112

Creamy White Bean and Anchovy Dip, 40, *41*
Cucumbers
 Salade Niçoise with Seared Tuna and White Beans, *48*, 51

D
Demi-sec beans, 10, 17
Dips. see Spreads, dips, and appetizers
Duck
 Cassoulet, More-or-Less Toulouse-Style, 94, 98–99, *99*
 Duck Breast, Lentil, and Green Herb Salad, 60
 Garbure, 118
 A Grand Cassoulet with Lamb, Pork, and Duck Confit, 96–97
 Périgord-Style Duck Soup with White Beans, *120*, 121
 Slightly Short-Cut Cassoulet, 100, *101*

E
Eggs, hard-boiled
 Classic Salade Niçoise, 52
 Salade Niçoise with Seared Tuna and White Beans, *48*, 51
English peas
 Springtime Soupe au Pistou, 107
Entrées. see Gratins, roasts, and other main dishes
Escudier, Jean-Noël, 49

F
Fall Soupe au Pistou, 108, *109*
Fennel
 Cream of Fennel and White Bean Soup, 112
Fish. see Anchovies; Herring; Salt cod; Sea bass; Smoked salmon; Smoked trout; Sole; Tuna
Flageolet beans
 about, 13, *12*
 lamb and, 71
 Lamb Stew with Flageolet Beans, 76, *77*
 Roast Leg of Lamb with Garlic, Herbs, and Flageolet Beans, *70*, 72–73, *73*
 Tomato-Braised Lamb Shanks with Flageolet Beans, 74–75, *75*
French green lentils. see Lentils

Fried Panisse Batons, 38
Frisée
    Sea Bass on a Bed of Puréed White Beans, 88, *89*

G

Garbure, 118
Garlic Shrimp with White Beans and Sauce Verte, 92, *93*
Goat Cheese and Green Lentil Spread With Chives, 35
A Grand Cassoulet with Lamb, Pork, and Duck Confit, 96–97
Gratins, roasts, and other main dishes, 69–101
    Basque-Style Beans with Standing Pork Rib Roast, 84–85, *85*
    Braised Chicken Thighs with Cranberry Beans and Basil, 83
    Cassoulet, More-or-Less Toulouse-Style, *94*, 98–99, *99*
    cassoulet, mystique of, 95
    Chickpea and Lamb Gratin with Harissa, 82
    Garlic Shrimp with White Beans and Sauce Verte, 92, *93*
    A Grand Cassoulet with Lamb, Pork, and Duck Confit, 96–97
    Gratin of Cranberry Beans, Sweet Peppers, and Toulose Sausage, *80*, 81
    Gratin of Leeks and White Beans with Gruyère, 78
    Hachis Parmentier, 79
    Lamb Stew with Flageolet Beans, 76, *77*
    lamb-and-flageolet love affair, 71
    Papillotes of Sole, White Beans, and Spinach with Saffron Sauce, *90*, 91
    Roast Leg of Lamb with Garlic, Herbs, and Flageolet Beans, *70*, 72–73, *73*
    Rosemary White Beans with Beef and Cherry Tomato Brochettes, *86*, 87
    Sea Bass on a Bed of Puréed White Beans, 88, *89*
    Slightly Short-Cut Cassoulet, 100, *101*
    Tomato-Braised Lamb Shanks with Flageolet Beans, 74–75, *75*
Green beans. *see* Haricots verts
Green bell peppers
    Classic Salade Niçoise, 52
    Salade Niçoise with Cranberry Beans and Tuna Confit, 50

Green Lentil and Goat Cheese Spread with Chives, 35
Green olives
    Grilled Calamari with Coco Beans and Charred Tomatoes, *64*, 65
Green onions
    Garlic Shrimp with White Beans and Sauce Verte, 92, *93*
    Grilled Calamari with Coco Beans and Charred Tomatoes, *64*, 65
Ground beef
    Hachis Parmentier, 79
Gruyère cheese
    Gratin of Leeks and White Beans with Gruyère, 78
    Hachis Parmentier, 79

H

Hachis Parmentier, 79
Ham. *see also* Prosciutto
    Garbure, 118
    Slightly Short-Cut Cassoulet, 100, *101*
Haricot de Soissons beans
    about, 13
    Haricots de Soissons Beans with Maroilles Cheese, 43
    White Beans with Arugula, Prosciutto, and Parmesan Vinaigrette, *58*, 59
Haricot Maïs du Béarn beans, 17
Haricots verts
    Classic Salade Niçoise, 52
    Classic Summer Soupe au Pistou, *104*, 106
    Couscous Garni, 114–115, *115*
    Fall Soupe au Pistou, 108, *109*
Harissa
    Chickpea and Lamb Gratin with Harissa, 82
    Couscous Garni, 114–115, *115*
Herring
    White Bean, Watercress, and Pickled Herring Salad, 54, *55*
Hill, Kate, 98
History of beans in France, 10–11
Hummus, Black Bean, 34

I

IGP (Indication Géographique Protégée) designation, 25
Italian sausages. *see* Toulouse sausages

J

Jambon cru
    Buttered Garlic Toasts with White Beans and Crispy Pork, 32, *33*

K

Kidney beans
    Salade Mexicaine, 62, *63*

L

Label Rouge, 25
Lamb
    Chickpea and Lamb Gratin with Harissa, 82
    Flageolet beans and, 71
    A Grand Cassoulet with Lamb, Pork, and Duck Confit, 96–97
    Lamb Stew with Flageolet Beans, 76, *77*
    Roast Leg of Lamb with Garlic, Herbs, and Flageolet Beans, *70*, 72–73, *73*
    Tomato-Braised Lamb Shanks with Flageolet Beans, 74–75, *75*
Lardons
    White Beans with Lardons, Red Peppers, and Piment d'Espelette, 56
Leeks
    Basque-Style Beans with Standing Pork Rib Roast, 84–85, *85*
    Cassoulet, More-or-Less Toulouse-Style, *94*, 98–99, *99*
    Classic Summer Soupe au Pistou, *104*, 106
    Fall Soupe au Pistou, 108, *109*
    Garbure, 118
    Gratin of Leeks and White Beans with Gruyère, 78
    Lamb Stew with Flageolet Beans, 76, *77*
    Périgord-Style Duck Soup with White Beans, *120*, 121
    Springtime Soupe au Pistou, 107
Lentils
    about, 21, 20
    Duck Breast, Lentil, and Green Herb Salad, 60
    Green Lentil And Goat Cheese Spread With Chives, 35
Lettuce. *see also* Salads
    Classic Salade Niçoise, 52
Lingot beans

about, 17–18
Basque-Style Beans with Standing Pork Rib Roast, 84–85, *85*
Breton Beans, 119
Cassoulet, More-or-Less Toulouse-Style, *94*, 98–99, *99*
Creamy White Bean and Anchovy Dip, 40, *41*
Garbure, 118
A Grand Cassoulet with Lamb, Pork, and Duck Confit, 96–97
Gratin of Leeks and White Beans with Gruyère, 78
Grilled Calamari with Coco Beans and Charred Tomatoes, *64*, 65
Loubia, 110, *111*
Périgord-Style Duck Soup with White Beans, *120*, 121
Salade Niçoise with Seared Tuna and White Beans, *48*, 51
Slightly Short-Cut Cassoulet, 100, *101*
Smoked Salmon and White Bean Rillettes, 42
Smoked Trout, Shaved Celery, and White Beans with Tarragon Vinaigrette, 61
Springtime Soupe au Pistou, 107
White Bean, Watercress, and Pickled Herring Salad, 54, *55*
Lingot de Lauragais (Lingot de Castelnaudary) beans, 18
Lingot de Mazères beans, 18
Lingot du Nord beans
　about, 18
　Carbonnade with Lingot du Nord Beans, 116, *117*
Loubia, 110, *111*

M

Main dishes. *see* Gratins, roasts, and other main dishes
Maroilles Cheese, Haricots de Soissons Beans with, 42
Médecin, Jacques, 49
Merguez sausages
　Couscous Garni, 114–115, *115*
Mexican-style salad, 62, *63*
Mogette de Vendée beans
　about, 18
　Buttered Garlic Toasts with White Beans and Crispy Pork, 32, *33*

Carbonnade with Lingot du Nord Beans, 116, *117*
Munster cheese
　Haricots de Soissons Beans with Maroilles Cheese, 43

N

Niçoise olives
　Classic Salade Niçoise, 52, 53
　Salade Niçoise with Seared Tuna and White Beans, *48*, 51

O

Olives. *see* Black olives; Green olives; Niçoise olives
Orange bell peppers
　Gratin of Cranberry Beans, Sweet Peppers, and Toulouse Sausage, *80*, 81

P

Pain de campagne
　Carbonnade with Lingot du Nord Beans, 116, *117*
Pain d'épices
　Carbonnade with Lingot du Nord Beans, 116, *117*
Pancetta
　Cassoulet, More-or-Less Toulouse-Style, *94*, 98–99, *99*
　Garbure, 118
　Slightly Short-Cut Cassoulet, 100, *101*
Panisse
　chickpeas in, 21
　Fried Panisse Batons, 38
Papillotes of Sole, White Beans, and Spinach with Saffron Sauce, *90*, 91
Parmesan cheese
　Hachis Parmentier, 79
　White Beans with Arugula, Prosciutto, and Parmesan Vinaigrette, *58*, 59
Parsley
　Chickpea Beignets, *44*, 45
　Garlic Shrimp with White Beans and Sauce Verte, *92*, 93
　Hachis Parmentier, 79
　Tomato-Braised Lamb Shanks with Flageolet Beans, 74–75, *75*
Peas
　Springtime Soupe au Pistou, 107

Peppers. *see* Bell peppers; Red peppers
Périgord-Style Duck Soup with White Beans, *120*, 121
Pickled Herring Salad, White Bean, Watercress, and, 54, *55*
Pig's feet
　Cassoulet, More-or-Less Toulouse-Style, *94*, 98–99, *99*
　A Grand Cassoulet with Lamb, Pork, and Duck Confit, 96–97
Pois chiches. *see* Chickpeas
Pork. *see also* Bacon; Ham; Merguez sausages; Pancetta; Pig's feet; Prosciutto; Toulouse sausages
　Basque-Style Beans with Standing Pork Rib Roast, 84–85, *85*
　Buttered Garlic Toasts With White Beans And Crispy Pork, 32, *33*
　Cassoulet, More-or-Less Toulouse-Style, *94*, 98–99, *99*
　A Grand Cassoulet with Lamb, Pork, and Duck Confit, 96–97
Potatoes
　Classic Salade Niçoise, 52
　Classic Summer Soupe au Pistou, *104*, 106
　Fall Soupe au Pistou, 108, *109*
　Garbure, 118
　Salade Niçoise with Seared Tuna and White Beans, *48*, 51
　Springtime Soupe au Pistou, 107
Prosciutto. *see also* Ham
　Buttered Garlic Toasts with White Beans and Crispy Pork, 32, *33*
　Chickpeas with Prosciutto, Black Olives, and Cherry Tomatoes, *66*, 67
　White Beans with Arugula, Prosciutto, and Parmesan Vinaigrette, *58*, 59

R

Radicchio
　Salad of Salt Cod and White Beans, 57
Ragout of Chickpeas and Chorizo, 113
Red peppers. *see also* Bell peppers
　Chickpea and Lamb Gratin with Harissa, 82
　Fall Soupe au Pistou, 108, *109*
　Gratin of Cranberry Beans, Sweet Peppers, and Toulouse Sausage, *80*, 81
　Lamb Stew with Flageolet Beans, 76, *77*

Salade Mexicaine, 62, *63*
White Beans with Lardons, Red Peppers, and Piment d'Espelette, 56
Rice
Springtime Soupe au Pistou, 107
Rillettes, smoked salmon and white bean, 42
Roast Leg of Lamb with Garlic, Herbs, and Flageolet Beans, *70*, 72–73, *73*
Roasts. *see* Gratins, roasts, and other main dishes
Rosemary
Basque-Style Beans with Standing Pork Rib Roast, 84–85, *85*
Roast Leg of Lamb with Garlic, Herbs, and Flageolet Beans, *70*, 72–73, *73*
Rosemary White Beans with Beef and Cherry Tomato Brochettes, *86*, 87
Tomato-Braised Lamb Shanks with Flageolet Beans, 74–75, *75*
Royal Corona beans
Cream of Fennel and White Bean Soup, 112
Creamy White Bean and Anchovy Dip, 40, *41*
Gratin of Leeks and White Beans with Gruyère, 78
Hachis Parmentier, 79
Haricots de Soissons Beans with Maroilles Cheese, 43
Rosemary White Beans with Beef and Cherry Tomato Brochettes, *86*, 87
Sea Bass on a Bed of Puréed White Beans, *88*, 89
White Bean And Chorizo Tartines, *36*, 37
White Beans with Arugula, Prosciutto, and Parmesan Vinaigrette, *58*, 59

S

Salade Niçoise, 48–53
about, 49
Classic Salade Niçoise, 52
with Cranberry Beans and Tuna Confit, 50
with Seared Tuna and White Beans, *48*, 51
Salads, 46–67
Chickpeas with Prosciutto, Black Olives, and Cherry Tomatoes, *66*, 67
Classic Salade Niçoise, 52
Duck Breast, Lentil, and Green Herb Salad, 60
Grilled Calamari with Coco Beans and Charred Tomatoes, *64*, 65
Salad of Salt Cod and White Beans, 57
Salade Mexicaine, 62, *63*
Salade Niçoise: From Simple Southern Meal to International Favorite, 49
Salade Niçoise with Cranberry Beans and Tuna Confit, 50
Salade Niçoise with Seared Tuna and White Beans, *48*, 51
Smoked Trout, Shaved Celery, and White Beans with Tarragon Vinaigrette, 61
White Bean, Watercress, and Pickled Herring Salad, 54, *55*
White Beans with Arugula, Prosciutto, and Parmesan Vinaigrette, *58*, 59
White Beans with Lardons, Red Peppers, and Piment d'Espelette, 56
Salmon, smoked
Cream of Fennel and White Bean Soup, 112
Smoked Salmon and White Bean Rillettes, 42
Salt Cod, and White Beans Salad, 57
Sando, Steve, 119
Sausages. *see* Merguez sausages; Toulouse sausages
Savoy cabbage
Garbure, 118
Périgord-Style Duck Soup with White Beans, *120*, 121
Sea Bass on a Bed of Puréed White Beans, *88*, 89
Shrimp
Garlic Shrimp with White Beans and Sauce Verte, *92*, 93
Slightly Short-Cut Cassoulet, 100, *101*
Smoked salmon
Cream of Fennel and White Bean Soup, 112
Smoked Salmon and White Bean Rillettes, 42
Smoked trout
Cream of Fennel and White Bean Soup, 112
Smoked Trout, Shaved Celery, and White Beans with Tarragon Vinaigrette, 61
Socca, 21
Soissons beans. *see* Haricot de Soissons beans
Sole
Papillotes of Sole, White Beans, and Spinach with Saffron Sauce, *90*, 91
Soupe au Pistou, 104–109
about, 105
Classic Summer Soupe au Pistou, *104*, 106
Fall Soupe au Pistou, 108, *109*
Springtime Soupe au Pistou, 107
Soups and stews, 102–121
Breton Beans, 119
Carbonnade with Lingot du Nord Beans, 116, *117*
Classic Summer Soupe au Pistou, *104*, 106
Couscous Garni, 114–115, *115*
Cream of Fennel and White Bean Soup, 112
Fall Soupe au Pistou, 108, *109*
Garbure, 118
Loubia, 110, *111*
Périgord-Style Duck Soup with White Beans, *120*, 121
Ragout of Chickpeas and Chorizo, 113
Soupe au Pistou, 104–109
Springtime Soupe au Pistou, 107
Spaghetti
Classic Summer Soupe au Pistou, *104*, 106
Fall Soupe au Pistou, 108, *109*
Spicy Roasted Chickpeas, 39
Spinach
Papillotes of Sole, White Beans, and Spinach with Saffron Sauce, *90*, 91
Spreads, dips, and appetizers, 30–45
Black Bean Hummus, 34
Buttered Garlic Toasts with White Beans and Crispy Pork, 32, *33*
Chickpea Beignets, *44*, 45
Creamy White Bean and Anchovy Dip, 40, *41*
Fried Panisse Batons, 38
Green Lentil and Goat Cheese Spread with Chives, 35
Haricots de Soissons Beans with Maroilles Cheese, 43
Smoked Salmon and White Bean Rillettes, 42

Spicy Roasted Chickpeas, 39
    White Bean and Chorizo Tartines, *36*, 37
Springtime Soupe au Pistou, 107
Squid
    Grilled Calamari with Coco Beans and Charred Tomatoes, *64*, 65

T

Tarbais beans
    about, 14, 15
    Basque-Style Beans with Standing Pork Rib Roast, 84–85, *85*
    Cassoulet, More-or-Less Toulouse-Style, 94, 98–99, *99*
    Cream of Fennel and White Bean Soup, 112
    Garbure, 118
    A Grand Cassoulet with Lamb, Pork, and Duck Confit, 96–97
    Hachis Parmentier, 79
    Loubia, 110, *111*
    Périgord-Style Duck Soup with White Beans, *120*, 121
    Rosemary White Beans with Beef and Cherry Tomato Brochettes, *86*, 87
    Salade Niçoise with Seared Tuna and White Beans, *48*, 51
    Sea Bass on a Bed of Puréed White Beans, 88, *89*
    Slightly Short-Cut Cassoulet, 100, *101*
    Smoked Trout, Shaved Celery, and White Beans with Tarragon Vinaigrette, 61
    White Bean And Chorizo Tartines, *36*, 37
    White Bean, Watercress, and Pickled Herring Salad, 54, *55*
Tomatoes
    Basque-Style Beans with Standing Pork Rib Roast, 84–85, *85*
    Braised Chicken Thighs with Cranberry Beans and Basil, 83
    Breton Beans, 119
    Chickpeas with Prosciutto, Black Olives, and Cherry Tomatoes, 66, *67*
    Classic Salade Niçoise, 52
    Fall Soupe au Pistou, 108, *109*
    A Grand Cassoulet with Lamb, Pork, and Duck Confit, 96–97
    Grilled Calamari with Coco Beans and Charred Tomatoes, *64*, 65
    Hachis Parmentier, 79

Lamb Stew with Flageolet Beans, 76, *77*
Loubia, 110, *111*
Rosemary White Beans with Beef and Cherry Tomato Brochettes, *86*, 87
Salade Niçoise with Cranberry Beans and Tuna Confit, 50
Salade Niçoise with Seared Tuna and White Beans, *48*, 51
Slightly Short-Cut Cassoulet, 100, *101*
Tomato-Braised Lamb Shanks with Flageolet Beans, 74–75, *75*
Toulouse sausages
    Cassoulet, More-or-Less Toulouse-Style, 94, 98–99, *99*
    A Grand Cassoulet with Lamb, Pork, and Duck Confit, 96–97
    Gratin of Cranberry Beans, Sweet Peppers, and Toulouse Sausage, *80*, 81
    Slightly Short-Cut Cassoulet, 100, *101*
Trout, smoked
    Cream of Fennel and White Bean Soup, 112
    Smoked Trout, Shaved Celery, and White Beans with Tarragon Vinaigrette, 61
Tuna
    Classic Salade Niçoise, 52
    Salade Niçoise with Cranberry Beans and Tuna Confit, 50
    Salade Niçoise with Seared Tuna and White Beans, *48*, 51
Turnips
    Couscous Garni, 114–115, *115*
    Garbure, 118
    Springtime Soupe au Pistou, 107

V

Ventriche
    Cassoulet, More-or-Less Toulouse-Style, 94, 98–99, *99*
Vilmorin, M., 10

W

Watercress
    White Bean, Watercress, and Pickled Herring Salad, 54, *55*
White beans. *see also* Alubia Blanca beans; Cannellini beans; Cassoulet beans; Lingot beans; Royal Corona beans; Tarbais beans
    Breton Beans, 119

Buttered Garlic Toasts with White Beans and Crispy Pork, 32, *33*
in cassoulet, 95
Cassoulet, More-or-Less Toulouse-Style, 94, 98–99, *99*
Classic Summer Soupe au Pistou, *104*, 106
Cream of Fennel and White Bean Soup, 112
Creamy White Bean and Anchovy Dip, 40, *41*
Fall Soupe au Pistou, 108, *109*
Garbure, 118
Gratin of Leeks and White Beans with Gruyère, 78
Grilled Calamari with Coco Beans and Charred Tomatoes, *64*, 65
Hachis Parmentier, 79
Loubia, 110, *111*
Papillotes of Sole, White Beans, and Spinach with Saffron Sauce, *90*, 91
Périgord-Style Duck Soup with White Beans, *120*, 121
Rosemary White Beans with Beef and Cherry Tomato Brochettes, *86*, 87
Salade Niçoise with Seared Tuna and White Beans, *48*, 51
Sea Bass on a Bed of Puréed White Beans, 88, *89*
Slightly Short-Cut Cassoulet, 100, *101*
Smoked Salmon and White Bean Rillettes, 42
Smoked Trout, Shaved Celery, and White Beans with Tarragon Vinaigrette, 61
White Bean And Chorizo Tartines, *36*, 37
White Bean, Watercress, and Pickled Herring Salad, 54, *55*
White Beans with Arugula, Prosciutto, and Parmesan Vinaigrette, *58*, 59
White Beans with Lardons, Red Peppers, and Piment d'Espelette, 56

Z

Zucchini
    Classic Summer Soupe au Pistou, *104*, 106
    Couscous Garni, 114–115, *115*

ACKNOWLEDGEMENTS

Not only did Steve Sando, founder and owner of Rancho Gordo, ask me if I'd like to write a book on French beans, he proposed taking the photos. Many thanks to Steve on both counts. Thank you to Julia Newberry for guiding this book from concept to conclusion, being on top of scheduling and details, as well as pinch-hitting as cook and photo stylist. To the lovely Sarah Scott, many thanks for cooking with me and sharing your skills and expertise on a long photo-shoot day at my house. We were also assisted by Cecilia Ortiz of Rancho Gordo — thank you to her. A special thank-you to Meghan Hildebrand for the design of the book, and, on our first photo shoot day, for her keen eye regarding props and photo styling. A big thank-you to our friends at Fatted Calf for supplying the excellent French-style meats and charcuterie, and to our friends at Elsie Green for the vintage French platters, dishes, and other tableware we used to supplement my own. To Ann Evans, thank you for the loan of your perfect white platters. No book should ever be published without a good copyeditor having gone over it thoroughly. For this important task, I especially thank Anita Epler Crotty for her excellent work. Last but not least, thank you to my husband, Jim Schrupp, for his enthusiastic tasting and critique of all the recipes in this book.